Developing Your Super Powers

This book is dedicated to those who love living, or want to.

Special Thanks and Acknowledgements:

Maryann Reese, LMFT, Southern Institute of NLP, Indian Rocks Beach, FL, for her excellent clinical consultation and patience.

My friends and family for their loving support in this long, but important, endeavor.

Quotes excerpted from *You Have a Purpose – Begin It Now*, Susan Hayward, Australia, In Tune Books

Developing Your Super Powers

Phenomenal Mind Powers You Don't Know You Have

Frances Williams Duncan, LCSW

IGP

Published by Inner Galaxies Press

DEVELOPING YOUR SUPER POWERS

Inner Galaxies Press
P.O. Box 2298
Tarpon Springs, FL 34688
www.innergalaxies.com
Toll Free 877-434-0005

Copyright © by Frances Williams Duncan 2002
ISBN 0-9722413-0-2
Library of Congress Control Number: 2002112441

All rights reserved, No part of this publication may be reproduced, stored in a retrieval system, or transmitted, in any form or by any means, electronic, mechanical, photocopying, recording or otherwise, without the prior permission of the publishers.

Table of Contents

Introduction   xi

Chapter 1. Exploring Your Inner Galaxies

Your Sleeping Strengths   1

What are Physical Memory Orgasms (PMOs)?   5

The Power in Your Brain's Pleasure/Pain Systems   7

NLP Techniques to Access Your Super Powers   10

Surprising Hormone Facts   17

Chapter 2. The Power of Beliefs and Your Subconscious Mind

Natural Phenomena – The Magic Within   25

The Power of Association – Your Gray Matter Matters   27

Challenging Your Limiting Beliefs   32

Assessing Your Limiting Beliefs Regarding Your Sexuality   36

Changing Limiting Beliefs   39

Chapter 3. Techniques for Physical Memory Orgasms

Steps to Access PMOs	43
Practice Physical Memory Accessing	61
Setting Your PMOs "Remote Control"	63
Super Power Techniques to Enhance Sex with Your Partner	66
Physical Limitations and Accessing PMOs	68

Chapter 4. Virtual Reality Fantasy

Virtual Reality Fantasy Techniques	71
Steps to Virtual Reality Fantasy	77
Virtual Reality Fantasy with Your Partner	82

Chapter 5. Relationship Super Powers

The Brain Chemistry of Love	83
Love/Relationship Addiction	86
The Stages of Love – Making It Last	91
Loving You	95

Chapter 6. Sexual Abuse and Physical Intimacy

The Effects of Sexual Abuse on Intimate Relationships   97

Steps to Dilute Sexual Abuse Trauma Responses   103

Untangling the Web of Love and Sex from Sexual Abuse   106

Chapter 7. Turning on Your Weight Loss Brain Chemistry

Setting Yourself Up for Success – A Therapeutic Approach to Weight Loss   109

How to Change Without Changing (Much)   116

The Smorgasbord Diet   120

Present Day Eating Patterns that Keep You Gaining   122

Assessing Your Eating Patterns   125

Deadly Roadblock Called Denial   130

Thin Americans – An Endangered Species?   133

Refuse to be Fat   134

Unique Super Power Techniques for Weight Loss   135

Nurturing Your Brain   152

Chapter 8. Developing Your Super Powers to Eliminate Addictions

Know What You Are Consenting to – Facts on Cigarette Smoking	155
The Brain Chemistry of Cigarette Smoking	158
Women Are at Greater Risk	159
Cigarette Smoking – A Major Factor in Infertility for Men and Women	160
Effects On An Unborn Child	161
Effects of Second Hand Smoke on Children	162
Cancer in All of Us?	163
Withdrawal – The Flip Side of the Coin	163
Why You Haven't Quit	165
Assessing Childhood Patterns/Associations that Keep You Hooked	169
Super Power Techniques to Stop Smoking	174
What If You Don't Want to Stop?	180
Indicators of Self-Neglect	182
Indicators of Self-Abuse	183

Choosing Happiness — 185

Anger Control Technique — 187

Chapter 9. Beyond the Physical

Creating Your Own Time Machine — 189

Time Travel Imagery Exercise — 192

Modern Science Anchors — 194

Forward Time Travel — 194

Accessing Your Subconscious Through Sleep and Dreams — 195

The Super Powers of Self-Healing — 198

What is Your Destiny? — 201

DEVELOPING YOUR SUPER POWERS

INTRODUCTION

When you think of Super Powers, you may think of comic book or movie super heroes who can do extraordinary things like fly, see through walls or leap tall buildings in a single bound. As human beings, our Super Powers may be less obvious, but no less impressive. We possess dormant Super Powers that may seem out of the realm of possibility now, but one hundred years from now may be commonplace.

Our subconscious mind holds claim to about 90% of our brainpower. Much of what we do happens automatically, with our subconscious mind at the wheel. You can learn to bring what you do subconsciously into your conscious awareness and discover talents and abilities you didn't know you had.

A Super Power is a phenomenal ability or skill that goes well beyond the average. A core Super Power that opens the door to others is learning how to access the pleasure systems of your brain with a mental command (thought) that releases naturally produced pleasure chemicals like dopamine and endorphins, among others. These pleasure chemicals are what we seek when we eat, have sex, smoke cigarettes, ride roller coasters, drink caffeine, and use alcohol or other drugs, including prescription medications for depression, anxiety or pain.

The skill to access your brain's pleasure systems with thought alone gives you the ability to choose your own brain chemistry naturally without putting harmful substances into your body, and without the negative consequences that happen with addictions. A chronic pain sufferer can learn to release endorphins (the brain's natural morphine) instantly. As you develop your Super Powers, your awareness will expand and you will develop control over mind-body processes that previously happened subconsciously.

You can learn Super Power techniques to naturally choose your brain chemistry to lose weight, stop smoking, increase sexual desire, stay (or return) to the "in love" stage of a romantic relationship, self-heal, reverse aging, activate your motivation, choose your moods, reduce sexual abuse trauma responses that can affect your sexual relationship(s), and have infinite orgasms at will, no sexual stimulation or fantasy required.

When you develop your Super Powers, you are recognizing and honing your innate abilities. One such innate ability is accessing Physical Memory Orgasms (PMOs). For women, PMOs occur by accessing *physical* memories of past sexual experiences resulting in very real unlimited multiple orgasms in the present. This is done through techniques that allow you to tap into your ability to instantly release natural pleasure brain chemicals any time you choose. Throughout this book, you will learn Physical Memory Accessing techniques that not only allow you to access Physical Memory Orgasms, but any desired state of mind.

Because of anatomical differences, men may not experience PMOs exactly the same way women do, but they can use the same techniques to extend and enhance their sexual experiences and orgasms, and learn to access their brain pleasure systems with thought for other purposes as well.

PMOs result in immediate physiological and scientifically measurable changes. These are the same physical changes and feelings that occur in your body and brain when you experience

Introduction

orgasms, because they are exactly that! A distinction between PMOs and orgasms in general is the ability to have effortless orgasms simply by deciding to, and having the ability to continue until you are ready to stop.

You can develop your own "remote control", along with a power button, rewind, pause, mute, turn up the volume and, of course, stop (darn). Not all orgasms are the same. You can choose what type of orgasms you wish to have and their level of intensity. You design your own buttons with your mind power. Once you learn the techniques to access PMOs and your other Super Powers, it will be as uncomplicated as yawning or scratching your nose.

Does it seem too good to be true? Does it sound sci-fi or futuristic? Remember the scene in the movie *Barbarella*, with Jane Fonda, where two people have an amazing sexual encounter in their brains by simply placing their hands together? Well, some of you already know how to do this, you just didn't tell the rest of us!

Theodore X. Barber, a hypnosis authority and altered states specialist at Cushing Hospital in Framingham, Massachusetts, did a controlled study and found that approximately 4% of the population, mostly women, can use sexual fantasy to reach orgasm with no physical stimulation (10). If you don't already have this skill, you are about to learn, and you don't even need sexual fantasy. However, fantasy can enhance Physical Memory Orgasms.

A Super Power that serves many purposes is Virtual Reality Fantasy (VRF). Virtual Reality Fantasy is what the name implies, fantasy experienced as real. The techniques used in VRF can intensify your PMOs and your sexual relationship with your partner. A male in a sexual relationship with a female who can access PMOs may find himself in for the sexual experiences of his lifetime, and possibly renew a relationship to the "honeymoon phase" that can keep it lasting. Men can access these naturally occurring brain chemicals by using the same techniques as women, and draw out or extend their orgasmic experiences.

Physical Memory Accessing, including Physical Memory Orgasms, is achieved through simple techniques that are a combination of Neuro-Linguistic Programming (NLP) and classical conditioning combined in a way that gives you the ability to activate the pleasure systems of your brain with thought. The primary focus of the techniques used in Physical Memory Accessing and PMOs is bringing into your conscious awareness what you do naturally on a subconscious level around the clock.

The elements that make Physical Memory Accessing and PMOs work can be found in the study of neuroscience, regarding how the brain works, how memory is stored and retrieved, how our senses of sight, sound, touch, smell and taste operate and how we learn.

There are endless benefits to having the ability to choose your brain chemistry naturally and access the pleasure systems of your brain at will. If you are trying to lose weight, stop smoking or eliminate any addiction, you probably know that willpower alone usually doesn't work. Willpower is a left brain function that relies on logic and reason. The right brain functions that trigger the pleasure systems of the brain, like our senses and emotions, fuel addictions. You can learn right brain approaches that give you the edge you have been missing in past attempts to lose weight or stop smoking.

Hormones play a crucial role in how our bodies function. A proper hormone balance aids in sexual functioning, health, mood and cognitive processes. Relationships are enhanced and can operate at their best with a good hormone balance. In this book, you will learn some facts on hormones and hormone replacement therapy options that may surprise you.

There is a reader survey enclosed at the end of this book designed so that readers may share their Super Power experiences and the present Super Power techniques can further evolve

Introduction

to help others. Also, the *Developing Your Super Powers Workbook* will further assist you in developing your skills.

I liken discovering PMOs, and the other techniques that help you develop your Super Powers, to finding a great recipe that few people have found. The ingredients already exist, but perhaps they haven't been blended in quite the same way before. Of course, as with any recipe, you have the creative freedom to add, subtract, or mix it up any way you choose and discover something that is completely and uniquely yours.

DEVELOPING YOUR SUPER POWERS

Chapter One
EXPLORING YOUR INNER GALAXIES

*Perhaps what we call genius
has something to do with
a learned state of consciousness,
a way of attending to the stream
of mental experience.*

*Perhaps many more of us could hear
inner melodies, find guidance
and inspiration, achieve
breakthrough insight —
if we would only pay attention to
the fleeting images and
the quiet intuitions presented to us
by the creative mind.*

Willlis Harmen

Your Sleeping Strengths

We live our lives without giving much thought to what we are made of, or more importantly, what we are really capable of. In their fascinating book, *The 3-Pound Universe*, Judith Hooper and Dick Teresi state the human brain could fit into the palm of a hand "but a computer with the same number of 'bits' would be 100 stories tall and cover the state of Texas." The number of brain cells it would take to make the size of a grain of sand would contain one hundred thousand neurons, two million axons and one billion synapses (16). The human brain has 100 billion cells, and the number of connections the brain can make is estimated to be more than the estimated number of atoms in the universe (11). Think about that the next time you question your capability of learning something new.

We also give little thought to the odds it took for us to get into this world. There are about 250 million sperm that are all vying for the same egg. No two human beings are exactly alike, past, present or future. Even clones would not have the same life experiences that influence whom we become.

We are hurling around in space at 65,000 miles per hour rotating around the sun that is 93 million miles away and is large enough to fit a million planets the size of earth inside of it (21). Our galaxy is just one of millions out there. How often do we think of the phenomena around us or within us?

The human brain has not physically changed much over the last 10,000 years. The caveman had the same basic brain structure that we have today. There was a 5,000 year gap between *having* our present thinking power and *using* it, as evidenced by the timing of the first cave drawings (10). What is changing about the human brain is not what's inside, but a greater conscious awareness of how to use what's there.

A consistent statement throughout the neuroscience literature is that we only use approximately 10% of our brainpower. The other 90% of self goes relatively unnoticed, but is our constant companion. The unconscious or subconscious parts of the brain continue to work for us whether we are aware of it or not. We get flashes of our subconscious mind when we dream, have gut instincts and when that voice inside us attempts to lead us in a particular direction.

The subconscious mind tends to be wiser than the conscious mind because it holds all of the accumulative experiences, thoughts and feelings that we have ever had and speaks to us from that wisdom. Usually when we ignore our inner voice, we end up regretting it. We have the answers within us to solve life's problems, but we sometimes have trouble trusting ourselves.

It makes sense that what we feed into our subconscious minds has a tremendous impact on us both physically and emotionally. The subconscious mind quietly guides us based on what information we have processed and the direction it receives from the conscious mind. Therefore, all input is significant, what we watch on television or at the movies, the music we listen to, what we read, what others say to us, what we say to others, what we think during the day and so on. All this changes our brain chemistry while it is occurring. Everything we experience goes into our subconscious mind and directly influences our lives over time.

Have you ever been mulling over where you are going to eat for lunch and find yourself driving in the direction of a particular restaurant before you think you have even made up your mind? In his book *The Learning Brain*, Eric Jensen states, "Two researchers, Pfurtscheller and Berghold, verified that as early as two seconds prior to an actual activity or movement, your brain has already decided what body parts to activate and which side of the brain to use. This means you are already acting on something before you are truly aware that you are even thinking about it."

We have shifts of awareness, depending on our activities. You may have a headache or some other physical or emotional discomfort and need to focus your attention elsewhere, perhaps on work or handling a crisis, and your attention will be drawn away from your pain and discomfort. The moment you are able to get back in touch with yourself, you are once again acutely aware of how you are feeling. Your pain and discomfort didn't go anywhere. You simply weren't able to pay attention to it for a short period of time.

The human brain produces electrical energy that fluctuates in rhythms. These rhythms are measured in cycles per second. Regardless of our activities, we have regular cycles of daydreams throughout our wake time. When we watch television, listen to music, read, drive, listen to someone talk when we aren't really listening, and when we are doing mundane chores, we are often in a trance state. Our electrical brain wave patterns cycle slower when we are in a "trance". These are just a few situations when our level of conscious awareness may wane. These are also the times we are more susceptible to any outside influence whether it is direct or indirect, like commercials and advice from friends.

A person who is prone to anxiety may have electrical brain wave patterns that cycle quickly, putting them into a hyper-alert state that interferes with their ability to rest, sleep or feel calm. What we eat and drink or any substances or medications we use can certainly affect our brain's electrical energy cycles.

The electrical energy the brain produces changes depending on our level of conscious awareness. The slower brain rhythms (alpha waves) are experienced just before going to sleep, when we first wake up, when we are daydreaming, or during hypnosis and meditation. Any activity that produces alpha waves gives us the most direct route to the subconscious mind.

Retrieving information from your subconscious and bringing it into your conscious awareness can give you access to inherent strengths and abilities you didn't know existed. The techniques presented here are designed to help you explore your inner galaxies, develop your Super Powers and enrich your life.

What Are Physical Memory Orgasms?

Learning to access Physical Memory Orgasms (PMOs) is an exciting and life-enhancing experience into uncharted territory. I encourage you to take your time and enjoy the journey.

Learning to access PMOs is a process and one skill builds on the next. You may be tempted to peek ahead, and that wouldn't hurt, but you will have better results if you read each chapter in sequence.

Physical Memory Orgasms and Physical Memory Accessing of any past experience is recalling physical sensations (body memories) of both mind and body of a past experience and bringing that physiological experience into the present. In turn, the brain chemicals released will be the same brain chemistry you experienced at the time of the original event. This ability gives you the power to choose your brain chemistry with thought alone, and gives you control over mind-body processes that previously happened subconsciously.

Physical Memory Orgasms are more than simply remembering past orgasmic experiences. PMOs are *actual* physical orgasms in the present experienced by accessing *physical* memories of orgasm(s) or sexual experiences you have had in the past. After you have learned how to do this naturally and easily, it will be a matter of remembering the physical mechanisms of orgasm itself (what happens in your body and brain during orgasm) rather than recalling a specific memory of an orgasm.

If I asked you to remember a burp and burp now (try it), you wouldn't necessarily have to remember the burp you had on Thanksgiving Day in 1995, but what you do physically with your body to burp anytime. When you have learned to access PMOs with ease, you can skip the in-between steps and go directly to PMOs with no thought, sexual or otherwise, except to decide it's what you want to do, and you can do it as easily as burping.

The release of the natural pleasure brain chemicals happens instantly. There are also no limits on how many times, for how long, or how often you can do this and get the same results, except self limits such as situational circumstances, or getting too tired to continue. Is this a new category for Guinness?

An additional benefit of accessing PMOs is effortless and pleasurable workouts of the buttocks and lower abdominal muscles, and strengthening of the vaginal muscles. You have probably heard of the Kegel exercises for females that can strengthen your PC (pubococcygial) muscle to improve orgasm. This is the muscle that stops the flow of urine in both men and women. The benefits of PMOs go well beyond those of Kegel exercises. You will find with PMOs there is no better exercise for vaginal muscles than the muscle contractions of orgasm.
Not only does it tighten the inside of the vagina, it strengthens the PC muscle and improves the quality and quantity of orgasms. Exercise may take on a whole new meaning.

You may worry that you would overuse such a talent. In the beginning you may be so excited with this fascinating ability that you keep testing it. Of course, who doesn't want to feel like *that*? This doesn't mean, however, that you will become so preoccupied with PMOs that it dominates your life. Life demands our attention.

Think back to a time you were madly in love, and you would rather make love than eat or sleep. You may remember that eventually you had to get back to work and do the other things you do everyday. It works the same with PMOs.

After you become proficient in accessing PMOs, and your other Super Powers, they become a natural part of you just like the many other things you know how to do. The difference is your level of consciousness will be on a much higher plane, and you will have the ability to choose your brain chemistry naturally and enhance numerous aspects of your life. Learning to access PMOs is **not** recommended for anyone struggling with a sexual addiction, for obvious reasons.

The Power in Your Brain's Pleasure/Pain Systems

In learning how to access the pleasure systems of the brain, it may be helpful to know how these systems operate and how they affect our daily lives. The limbic system of the brain houses our pain/pleasure and emotional systems. Our genetically built in need for survival is also linked to the limbic system. Basically, the pain and pleasure systems of the brain encourage us to do the things that will preserve our species, like having sex and eating, and discourage us from doing things that would get us hurt or killed. We have a built in reward and punishment system that reinforces good choices and discourages potentially dangerous ones.

If you feel pain, you are not feeling much pleasure and if you are feeling pleasure, you may not be aware of much pain. Think of it as a coin. Heads is pleasure and tails is pain. The coin can only land on one side at a time. When you have the ability to access pleasure at will (a guarantee of the coin always landing on heads), you can dampen the pain system as a result. This includes emotional pain as well as physical pain. You will have more control and choice over your moods and emotions.

There is also a connection between aggression/violence and the pain/pleasure systems of the brain. James W. Prescott, Developmental Psychologist, National Institute of Child Health and Human Development, did research with Harlow monkeys that were intentionally deprived of stimulation such as touch and movement to learn about the effects of such deprivation on children. He learned that sensory deprivation damages the growing brain's emotional systems and essentially damages the pain/pleasure systems of the brain, as well.

The cerebellum, the part of the brain that is a command center for movement is also damaged if infants don't receive touch, nurturance and movement, like rocking. Dr. Prescott stated, "I'm now convinced that the root cause of violence is deprivation of physical pleasure. When you stimulate the neurosystems that mediate pleasure, you inhibit the systems that mediate violence; it's like a seesaw." (10).

How could being able to release the natural pleasure chemicals in the brain assist those on the higher end of the continuum of aggression and violence? One of the primary goals in learning anger management techniques is developing internal control. When you can release feel good brain chemicals by deciding to, you have an increased level of self-control. Using this skill can place anger, violence and aggression on the low end of the seesaw.

The effects of abuse and trauma are emotional and physical, and can result in actual physiological changes in the brain. A childhood filled with abuse, trauma and neglect can train the brain to stay in a chronic state of alarm. As an adult, the person who has this history can walk around in day to day life with the brain chemistry an average person would have if their house were on fire. Needless to say, if you have this predominant brain chemistry, it doesn't take much to trigger a hyper-alarm state. What can seem trivial to most can seem catastrophic to you. This chronic alarm state results in hypervigilance and anxiety.

Every mood, thought, emotion or any state of mind has an accompanying mix of brain chemicals, or a brain chemistry "cocktail", that occurs when we are in that state of mind. There is a different set of brain chemicals released when we feel anxious (i.e., cortisol) than when we feel calm. A feeling of happiness results in an increase in serontonin, dopamine, and endorphins. When these pleasure brain chemicals are at a low, we may feel sad or depressed.

When we repeatedly experience excessive sadness, anxiety, anger, etc., as we grow and develop, neurological pathways become engrained and emotional patterns are formed that stay with us throughout our lives, until we learn to recognize them and change them. (More on this in Chapter 8.) Throughout this book you will learn techniques that will enable you to develop the Super Power ability to choose your brain chemistry with thought.

The potential connections that exist in the brain during the early stages of development are too many to calculate. The more enrichment, love and nurturance a child receives the more connections they make and keep for life, including more connections in the pleasure systems of the brain. Without it, cells die off and windows of opportunity can be lost forever.

We each have our own unique brain map that reflects how we organize input. No two are alike, human or other animal. Our maps keep changing by our continued development throughout life, what we put into our brains (daily choices), and what we experience from moment to moment. We affect our own brain chemistry continuously by what we think, how we behave and what we put into our bodies.

We continue to learn regardless of age. Enrichment counts no matter how old or young we are. When we learn something new, connections are formed in just a few seconds, like right now while you are reading this book!

Researchers at Yale University Center for Behavioral Medicine found that reading a book for half an hour a day changes the brain physically in the same way Transcendental Meditation does (10). If we are reading something we find interesting or challenging, this increases adrenaline, leaving us with a feeling of anticipation and excitement.

Another area of research regarding learning was done at Duke University. Studies show that sex helps you learn and remember more. The brain chemicals that are produced during sex help brain cells grow and produce new dendrites (44). The more dendrites we have, the greater our capacity to learn. PMOs release these same brain chemicals.

Ninety-nine percent of learning is unconscious. Our brains

are constantly taking in information through our senses, processing it and storing it for future reference. We can choose what goes into our heads in most instances and, therefore, already have the ability to change our brain chemistry at will (more on this later). If we don't know we have the ability to choose our brain chemistry, we tend to leave it up to happenstance and often feel out of control of our own lives.

NLP Techniques to Access Your Super Powers

The techniques to access PMOs include Neuro-Linguisitic Programming (NLP) techniques. The NLP techniques that are relevant to accessing PMOs and your other Super Powers will be introduced as they become applicable.

NLP started in the early 1970's with the work of John Grinder, who was an Assistant Professor of Linguistics at the University of California, Santa Cruz, and Richard Bandler, who was a Psychology student at the University during that time (14).

The **Neuro** in Neuro-Linguistic Programming conveys that all behavior stems from our neurological processes including sight (visual), hearing (auditory), smell (olfactory), taste (gustatory) and touch (kinesthetic). Smell, taste and touch are generally grouped together under kinesthetic in terms of modes of learning. Unless there is impairment in one or more senses, we use all five senses to process and store information (memory) about the world and our experiences. But, we usually have one sense that is our primary mode of learning.

If someone reads to you from the newspaper and you ask to see it instead; or, if you have problems following written instructions when putting something together but could do it easily if you see it done, you are probably a visual learner.

If you take in and retain information best from lectures or tapes, you may be primarily an auditory learner.

If you need to touch/smell/taste things to experience them,

and you are a person who automatically reaches out physically to others, you are most likely a kinesthetic learner.

It is important to keep these differences in mind if you are a parent or work with children. Imagine a kinesthetic learner in a classroom. Touching and smelling things might get a little boy or girl into a lot of trouble. Of course, touching, smelling and putting things into their mouths are also developmentally normal behaviors for infants and toddlers. This is how they learn about their world. All this sensory information is stored in the unconscious mind. It is the foundation that our later experiences are filtered through.

We experience the world through our five senses. Then, we process the information and act on it. What often gets us into trouble is a tendency to think and act as if our way of integrating information, processing it and acting on it is THE way. We may not necessarily think that everyone has to do it our way, but we may not recognize that someone else's experience of the same event is different than our own.

At one of my son's soccer games recently, one of the mothers walked up to me and said, "I can't stand behind the other team's parents anymore when I'm watching the game." When I asked her why, she said, "It's like we are watching two different games. They are seeing something completely different than I am seeing, and it's hard not to say something." The same game but different perceptions.

In *The 3-Pound Universe* famed scientist Candace B. Pert states, "Freud was right about the unconscious. In studying the way the brain processes information, we've learned much never reaches consciousness. As input from the senses percolates up to higher levels of the nervous system, it gets processed at each stage. Some is discarded; some is passed on to higher brain regions. There's a filtering, a selection, based on emotional meaning, past meaning, and so on." Candace Pert discovered the opiate receptor in the brain in 1973, opening the doorway for better understanding of how the pleasure/pain systems of the brain work and, consequently, the improved development of medications for mood disorders and mental illness. A receptor is what a brain chemical attaches to for its effect. You might think of it as an electrical outlet that a brain chemical "plugs" into. Candace Pert's statement explains individual perception.

All of our thoughts and feelings are processed through our individual "filters". Our actions are based on our perceptions. The cerebellum, pleasure/pain systems and other sensory processing areas are all part of one system. The mind-body connection makes PMOs possible. The brain's circuitry is an electrical system with direct wiring from the senses to the septum, or pleasure systems of the brain. Accessing PMOs turns on this switch.

Dr. Robert Heath, Tulane University Medical School, Department of Neurology and Psychiatry, began using implanted electrodes in the brains of patients with incurable epilepsy, Parkinson's disease, schizophrenia and severe pain in the early 1950's. The electrodes stimulated the pleasure center (septal area) of the brain turning off pain and turning on a feeling of pleasure. Dr. Heath and his associates took recordings from the pleasure/pain systems of the brain. Discussing pleasant topics would show pleasure systems firing. The punishment system would fire during rage attacks. In the 1970's, pacemakers were implanted in the brains of severely psychotic patients that were involved in the studies. The results were stunning. People who were institutionalized became able to function in society and, in some cases, live relatively normal lives (10).

This same group of researchers also found that when a neurotransmitter associated with memory (acetylcholine), was injected into a patient's septal area, the patient reported intense pleasure with multiple orgasms going on for over thirty minutes. Accessing PMOs obviously stimulates the septal region of the brain, but no electrodes are needed, just your own knowhow.

The **Linguistic** element of Neuro-Linguistic Programming relates to how we use words and language to think and communicate. Words have different meanings to different people. The word "love" is a good example. As a licensed psychotherapist, I have learned that one of the most common problems with couples in treatment for couple's counseling is poor communication. One or both partners may not feel loved in the relationship, and they often have difficulty expressing or even identifying their needs.

A couple I worked with several years ago is a classic example. Her idea of love was romance, surprises, dancing and candlelight. His idea of love was working very hard to support and provide for his family. He didn't *feel* loved by her because she didn't take care of him or the family by doing the laundry promptly and keeping the house clean. He didn't understand why she didn't know he loved her very much. After all, he worked seventy plus hours a week to provide for her and the children. She didn't *feel* loved because they never went out, and surprising her with flowers or a card didn't occur to him.

The **Programming** in Neuro-Linguistic Programming refers to the way we process information and how we act on it. This couple was in marriage counseling because she was considering a divorce. The fighting, and ultimately the counseling, was their way of acting on how they were processing information about each other and their relationship. Through the counseling, they discovered that they, in effect, spoke different languages and learned how to express their needs in a way the other could better respond to and understand. NLP techniques can be used in psychotherapy, communication, and used to access PMOs.

It is important to note in the definition of Physical Memory Orgasms, that the term used was *physical* memory. When you use Physical Memory Accessing and access PMOs, you go beyond just remembering or thinking about an experience. You bring into the present the physical memories from an earlier experience, and those physiological changes reoccur in the present. Our memories are stored with these sensory experiences.

For example, think about what peanut butter looks like. Do you see it? What color is it? What does peanut butter smell like? Oh, first you have to open the jar. How does that sound? What does peanut butter taste like? Now think about what peanut butter *feels* like when you get it stuck to the roof of your mouth, or when you try to swallow it. What does it *feel* like to step on a nail and have it go into your foot? What does it *feel* like to drink coffee that is too hot? Do you wince at the thought? What does it *feel* like to soak in a hot tub?

These are all physical memories, also called body memories. We have zillions of them. Generally our memories are remembered as a whole experience rather than a separation of the senses. The Techniques section in Chapter 3 will teach you how to recall physical memories by using your separate senses.

We are all familiar with how a favorite song can bring back memories, and make you feel as though you are "there" now. Hearing music we like can produce endorphins that make us feel good. Hearing music we find irritating can release stress chemicals like cortisol and produce anxiety (6). Hearing a song that triggers memories of a past love can transfer you back in time momentarily. Learning to develop a conscious awareness of how your five senses and memory work is instrumental in accessing PMOs.

Smell is the strongest of the senses in terms of memory. Smells have the potential to create intense feelings, erotic and otherwise. The olfactory (smell) bulb is in the middle of the limbic system. The olfactory nerve fibers go directly to the memory and emotion centers of the brain in a direct route. Visual information makes stops along the way. The olfactory area is filled with endorphin receptors. Smells you identify as positive release endorphins and change your brain chemistry to pleasure.

Our sense of smell also plays a major role in physical attraction. The subtle scent of pheromones released by males and females can trigger sexual arousal, especially when the chemistry is right. Dr. Theresa L. Crenshaw in *The Alchemy of Love and Lust* states, "Each and every one of us has a 'smell print'. In fact, every square centimeter of skin sloughs off one thousand cells per hour, leaving our individual smell print behind."

Three pheromones that affect sexual attraction are androstenol, androstenone and copulins. Both men and women have androstenol and androstenone, but only women have copulins. Copulins are found in vaginal secretions and have been shown in studies to increase testosterone in males. The limitless multiple orgasms of PMOs will increase vaginal secretions which in turn increase copulins. He may never know what hit him.

The power of sensory memory is evident in the treatment of sexually abused children and adults. Most people who've experienced this kind of trauma have symptoms of Post Traumatic Stress Disorder (PTSD) such as nightmares, flashbacks and hypervigilance.

A flashback is an intense memory of the trauma. The person can feel as if it is happening to them right now, both physically and emotionally. Anything that reminds them of the trauma can trigger a flashback, especially smells. A person sexually abused in a musty basement can re-experience the trauma, with all the sensory acuity felt at the time, if he or she smells an odor similar to a musty basement.

Any of your senses activated in the present can send you back in time with the same brain chemistry you experienced then. The principle is the same whether it is a precious memory or haunting one. As you are learning to access PMOs and your other Super Powers, you will learn simple techniques that will instantly take you to any desired state of mind, including orgasm, with the accompanying physiological changes. You can learn to *choose* your brain chemistry naturally to facilitate weight loss, have the brain chemistry of smoking without the cigarettes, healing, happiness and serenity, self-confidence, or whatever state of mind you are seeking.

You have probably heard or used the expression "Don't even go there," in reference to bringing up a topic someone doesn't want to hear or discuss. This statement implies there is a place to go. This place is referred to in Self Organization Theory as a basin. In actuality, memories are not in one location but are stored throughout the brain. Maybe this is nature's insurance policy.

Some basins are deep and broad while others of less significance may be smaller and shallower. The concept of basins in how we store memories is also important in working with trauma. A trauma basin can be very deep and wide. As human beings we naturally go to the deepest, widest basin even if it is negative. This can explain why it can be hard to change behaviors even if they are self-destructive.

It's like getting your car stuck deep in the mud or snow. The more you spin your wheels, the deeper you become entrenched and the harder it is to get out. Your tires are drawn back into the deepest hole. Specific Super Power techniques for reducing the intensity and magnitude of a trauma basin are described in Chapter 6.

Of course, we also have deep and wide basins for positive experiences. Accessing PMOs is going to the basins of the pleasure systems of the brain, deepening those basins, and learning to experience them in the present any time at your discretion.

The human brain stores information by categories, much like a filing system. If you were asked to list everything you remember and associate with dogs, how many memories could you recall? When we discuss how to retrieve physical memories to access PMOs, categories become very important.

Surprising Hormone Facts

Discovering PMOs is the result of a combination of professional training, experience as a licensed psychotherapist and personal life experiences. The following is about one of those personal life experiences.

In my late thirties, I began to experience perimenopausal symptoms. Perimenopause is called "the change before the change." It can occur even earlier than the late thirties. Perimenopause includes symptoms of heavy bleeding, hot flashes, night sweats, sleep disturbances, irritability, anxiety, forgetfulness, severe PMS, depression and poor concentration. Perimenopause progresses into menopause. The length of time for this transition varies.

I had many "female" surgeries, including removal of one ovary. The symptoms worsened and my doctor eventually recommended a hysterectomy. He asked if I wanted to keep my remaining ovary or have it removed. I told him I wasn't sure, I just knew I didn't want any more surgeries. He said he would remove the ovary. That decision turned out to be a tremendous mistake for me. I had no way of knowing that this simple verbal exchange with my doctor would change my life so negatively and drastically.

After surgery I had an IV pump that administered pain medication at the push of a button. The only problem was I threw up within seconds of pushing it and felt very drugged. At that time, I didn't know how to access the natural painkillers my body produces and tap into my own well of endorphins as easily and quickly as pushing the button on the pump.

I learned the hard way that women who go through surgical menopause (hysterectomy) lose estrogen and testosterone suddenly and dramatically. Testosterone levels can drop significantly within 24-48 hours after a hysterectomy. Some estrogen and testosterone are still stored in the fatty tissues of your body the first couple of weeks, and the effects aren't felt immediately.

Estrogen keeps vaginal infections at bay. Without estrogen, the PH balance becomes imbalanced and bacteria thrive resulting in frequent vaginal infections. I only recently learned a lack of estrogen worsens interstitial cystitis (6), a very painful bladder disease I have had for 26 years. Having sex the years following the surgery was comparable to eating my favorite ice cream with glass in it. Besides pain, there was a sense of loss and a feeling of being defective.

Testosterone is the hormone that affects the sex drive in both men and women. Women have much lower testosterone levels than men, but this isn't equivalent to a lower sex drive. Women require smaller amounts of testosterone for the same or greater results. A small amount of testosterone is produced in the adrenal glands, but testosterone is primarily produced in the ovaries of females and the testes of males. HRT offered to women after a hysterectomy rarely includes testosterone.

I discovered I was unable to tolerate hormone replacement therapy (HRT). I wrongly assumed everyone could take hormone replacements, and my doctor didn't advice me otherwise. When I took estrogen, I felt as though I had PMS everyday of my life. Over the next five years I tried every combination, brand and method that was recommended to me, but nothing helped. I tried different doctors without success.

There are other hormones and important brain chemicals that are affected by a decrease or loss of estrogen and testosterone. One such brain chemical is oxytocin. Oxytocin is the peptide (message carrier) in both men and women that help them bond, and it is produced in response to any positive touch, sexual or otherwise.

Women tend to have a stronger need for loving touch as a prelude to sexual touch. This is related to how oxytocin works in synchrony with estrogen. Without estrogen, oxytocin loses its punch for women. One can lose the desire to be touched, sexual or otherwise. Oxytocin is also the peptide that bonds parent and child and gives our skin its sensitivity to touch. Oxytocin reaches it's highest level during orgasm (6). PMOs increase oxytocin, as well as many other desirable hormones that will be discussed as they relate.

Another significant pleasure brain chemical that is influenced by testosterone and estrogen and has a starring role in romantic relationships is PEA (phenylethylamine). PEA gives us that "in love" feeling, and it is a natural amphetamine produced by our bodies. It gives us that giddy, excited feeling of infatuation. PEA works as an antidepressant and can work like a diet pill, decreasing appetite. Remember how you didn't want to eat or sleep when you first feel in love? That was the bonfire of PEA and, since PEA also peaks during orgasm, you were probably fueling that fire. PEA also rises at ovulation (6).

An absence of estrogen and testosterone can affect individuals and relationships. Massive amounts of hurt, blame, guilt and anger can build. Even the once most loving couples can find themselves with too much distance between them to bridge.

I had given up on HRT until I heard about hormone implants on the nightly news. At least it was different, something I had not tried. Still, I was hesitant and I didn't call for a few more months. Part of my reluctance was my previous tries with HRT and the side effects. I was worried that with implants I wouldn't have the option of throwing them in the trashcan, but would be stuck until they wore off. I decided to go ahead, resolved that if this didn't work I would never try anything else again.

Edward Zbella, M.D., University Fertility Center, St. Petersburg and Clearwater, Florida, previously participated in a research project that used hormone implants. He was so impressed with the results that he continued to use them in his practice. Testosterone is FDA approved for pellet implants. Estradial is FDA approved but not in pellet implant form, at the present time. I signed a release giving permission for the implants.

An advantage of hormone implants over other forms of HRT is they give continuous and constant estrogen levels and bypass the liver. The benefits are generally greater and longer lasting. Estrogen in this form goes directly to the estrogen receptors in the brain and has a wonderful effect on the emotions. There is a gradual, slow release and your body and brain receives a consistent supply of the hormones, not a fluctuation of highs and lows that can be problematic with other forms of HRT.

Evelyn Kitka, ARNP, (to whom I will be forever grateful), performed the ten minute office procedure with no problem. The transformation began in just a few days. One of the first things I noticed was my predominant mood of irritability shifted to a feeling of contentment and happiness. I was revitalized. Rather than coming home from work and collapsing on the couch, I began to actually cook dinner and interact more with my family. My cognitive processing became clearer and sharper. My pre-hormone implants existence was reminiscent of looking through a camera lens that was out of focus.

Studies have shown that women who've had their ovaries removed and are without estrogen scored lower on cognitive tests. When they later received estrogen they regained all their cognitive skills. Estrogen also stimulates growth of dendrites and synapses in nerve cells in the brain (4).

The implants usually last from two to three months. It's easy to tell when they begin to wear off because I feel like Cinderella at the stroke of midnight. I've learned to schedule appointments before symptoms occur. The testosterone was increased to two pellets the second procedure and my black and white world turned to color again! Later I was able to reduce back to one testosterone pellet with the same results. Once I had my sexuality back, I began to add the techniques you will be reading about and PMOs were born.

There are many vital hormones the body produces that keep us physiologically young and feeling good. Many of these hormones increase during sex and orgasm. If you are female and you don't have adequate levels of estrogen, or if you don't have enough testosterone, regardless of gender, you probably won't have the desire for sex. This affects other hormones in your body as well.

DHEA is a hormone produced by both men and women. We have more DHEA than any other hormone in our body. DHEA increases sex drive, increases during orgasm, works as an antidepressant, promotes weight loss without eating less, improves cognition, improves the immune system, increases bone density and helps wounds heal, among other things. Alcohol, stress, obesity and oral contraceptives are some of the factors that decrease DHEA. DHEA is associated with longevity, and produces the pheromones that give us our own unique sexual attraction scent (6). Increasing your own natural DHEA has many advantages.

Growth Hormone is another primary hormone that decreases with age. It has many of the same benefits as DHEA and can increase sex drive. You can increase Growth Hormone by physical activity, sleeping and having adequate supplies of estrogen and testosterone. Dopamine and endorphins also increase Growth Hormone (6). PMOs give you the Super Power ability to access your natural supply of dopamine and endorphins when you choose. Accessing PMOs can do much more for you than make you feel the way orgasms make you feel. They set the wheels in motion for greater rewards. (More on these important brain chemicals in Chapter 6.)

By mid to late thirties a woman's level of testosterone decreases by more than half. Testosterone not only increases sexual drive in both genders, it enhances mood, acts as an antidepressant, improves concentration, increases energy, helps prevent osteoporosis and promotes increase in lean muscle in both men and women. Adding testosterone if there is not a deficiency, in either gender, will not give additional benefits, but can result in irritability or aggressive behavior.

Testosterone is converted into estradiol and has estrogen effects like improving calcium deposit in the bones, relieving hot flashes and improving sleep. This means testosterone can be a supply of estrogen for women who have not been able to tolerate other forms of estrogen replacement, though it replaces only a small amount.

Women may be concerned that their bodies will become masculine-like if they use supplemental testosterone. Excessive amounts of testosterone in women can result in extra hair growth, but not as it does in men. Your doctor should know what doses to prescribe that give you the maximum benefit with few or no side effects. Remember, women naturally produce testosterone. It is not strictly a male hormone.

Testosterone has been shown to reduce the growth cells lining the ducts in breast tissue, possibly reducing the risk of developing breast cancer. According to *Listening to Your Hormones* by Gillian Ford, "C.W. Lovell, M.D., has a menopause clinic in Baton Rouge, Louisiana, and has treated approximately 4,000 patients, almost exclusively with subdermal estradiol and testosterone pellets or with injections of estradiol and testosterone cyprionate. He found a marked statistical difference (a lower incidence than the national average) in the rates of breast cancer in his patients on testosterone."

There is a gradual decrease in testosterone for men as well as women as they age. Men can develop problems similar to women going through menopause. The common term for this is viropause. It generally occurs between the ages of 40 to 50, but can occur earlier or later. Viropause can occur gradually or happen suddenly. Impotency can be affected by lower DHEA levels, smoking cigarettes, and can be caused by various medications. Twenty-five percent of impotency is related to medications. You may be surprised to learn that prolonged use of nasal sprays can also cause impotency or premature ejaculation in men (6).

Other factors that can decrease sexual desire in women include prolactin (produced during breastfeeding) and progesterone in birth control pills. Progesterone is especially strong in Norplant (6). Many antidepressant medications cause a decrease in sexual desire and sexual functioning in both men and women. One antidepressant medication that is an exception to this is Wellbutrin. Wellbutrin may increase sexual desire (6).

If you are female and you are having any perimenopausal symptoms, going through menopause, have had a hysterectomy or are considering one, it is important to know all your options. Also note that all gynecologists do not perform hormone pellet implant procedures. Estrogen and testosterone implant pellets are made in a compound pharmacy. A compound pharmacist will have a list of physicians who perform the hormone implant procedure.

If you are male and are having symptoms of viropause, testosterone replacement therapy may be something you want to consider. Testosterone can be administered in many forms other than pellets, including oral, cream and injections.

It is essential to be your own informed health care advocate. Ask questions even if you are afraid or embarrassed, and always research and learn all you can about any medical procedure before you consent to it. If you are interested in learning more about hormone implants, consult with your physician. If that doesn't work, consult with someone else's physician.

DEVELOPING YOUR SUPER POWERS

Chapter Two

THE POWER OF BELIEFS AND YOUR SUBCONSCIOUS MIND

*How much longer will you
go on letting your energy sleep?
How much longer are you
going to stay oblivious of
the immensity of yourself?
Don't lose time in conflict;
lose no time in doubt —
Time can never be recovered and
if you miss an opportunity
it may take many lives before
another comes your way again.*

Bhagivan Shree Rajneesh

Natural Phenomena - The Magic Within

Untapped natural phenomena exist within us. We are born with more potential than we know how to use. We sometimes hear about accomplishments that seem to go beyond human capabilities. We've seen people walk on hot coals, and read about someone momentarily having super strength to lift a car off someone. Techniques such as biofeedback can be used to control blood pressure, change your heart rate and decrease pain, among other things.

When my younger son was in the hospital for asthma, he was hooked to a monitor that displayed his heart rate. The medications he is given for asthma are stimulants that increase heart rate. We would make a game out of his ability to decrease his heart rate through concentration to keep him occupied and more comfortable. He became very good at it. He was ten years old at the time.

Hypnosis can allow you direct access to your subconscious mind and the powers that lie within. When I began studying hypnotherapy I was very skeptical, but intrigued. Ed and Maryann Reese of the Southern Institute of NLP, Indian Rocks Beach, Florida, led the training I attended on hypnotherapy and NLP. The Reeses are Directors of International NLP, and once trained with the famed Hypnotherapist, Milton H. Erickson, M.D.

During the hypnotherapy training, Ed Reese asked if anyone had problems with chronic pain. He wanted to do a demonstration. Earlier, I had shared with him that I experience chronic pain, so he called on me. I was more than a little reluctant to volunteer. I thought hypnosis could work with most people, however, not with me. After some prompting, and with great hesitation, I finally participated in the demonstration.

Both Ed and Maryann are very charismatic people. I felt comfortable within a few minutes. The gist of the induction was to imagine my right hand in a bucket of ice and physically move my hand around in it. Ed wove his brand of magic and provided me with all the imagery I needed to be there.

A common myth about hypnosis is that you are asleep or unconscious during an induction. That myth isn't true. The feeling is similar to being engrossed in a good movie while someone is talking to you. You are vaguely aware someone is speaking to you, but your concentration is on your own sensory experiences.

Within moments my right hand became very cold and the rest of my body stayed warm. Once my hand was sufficiently cold, Ed asked me to place it on the area where the pain was and feel the cold penetrate through to relieve the pain. That was when I became a believer. It *was* like magic. It is difficult to give full credit to the experience. I just know my hand was truly freezing cold.

My brain gave a message to my body that my hand was cold through the imagery experience, and my body responded in kind. I placed my hand over the painful area, felt a cooling sensation, and the burning and pain went away.

I asked Ed in amazement how he did that. He replied that he didn't do it, I did. At the time, I didn't know what he meant. I do now. He guided me, but I used my mind power to make a physical change in my body that relieved me of pain. I can do it again anytime the pain returns. I wasn't given a fish. I was taught how to fish.

The Power of Association – Your Gray Matter Matters

In some of my earlier training in hypnotherapy, I saw a videotape of a woman who was allergic to anesthetic. She had three C-sections in her lifetime with only hypnosis for pain relief. Each of the surgeries was videotaped. She lay there smiling and singing while they operated on her. Having had two C-sections myself, it was difficult to fathom.

In the same training, I learned about a woman who had a deadly disease and the one medication that could help her could only be taken for a short time. The medication was lethal with long-term use. The doctors began to slowly wean her off the medication while using classical conditioning to extend the benefits of the medication by associating a particular smell and taste with each dose. (I don't recall the specific smell/taste, so to better illustrate we will say it was lemons.) She began to associate the smell and taste of lemons with her medication.

When her medication was stopped, her body responded as though she was still receiving the medication each time she smelled and tasted lemons. Her body became conditioned to respond through this classical conditioning. She was able to reap the benefits of the medication without putting the deadly substance into her body. This magic happens through a process called association. Of course, this woman was under professionally directed medical care. Follow your doctor's recommendations regarding prescribed medications.

The technique of association is key to accessing PMOs and developing your other Super Powers. Association and categorization are the brain's means of processing input and storing and retrieving memories and information.

Until her death several years ago, my grandmother baked me the most delicious custard pies when I visited her. The smell and taste of custard places me in my grandmother's kitchen where the room is filled with the enticing aroma of nutmeg. The association I make with custard is my grandmother's love. These memories triggered by the smell and taste of custard might explain why I can't buy a custard pie without eating the whole thing, even though the flavor is about one-tenth of one of her pies.

Think of a favorite food made by someone you love. What does it smell like? What does it taste like? What feelings do you associate with that particular food and why? Chapter 6 will help you explore your individual food associations, how these associations affect your eating habits today, and several unique techniques for weight loss.

We associate and categorize by naming our experiences and filing what we consider to be like experiences together. Stereotyping also happens in this way. Our brains are designed to process any new information through what already exists from previous experiences. We also tend to generalize information.

(i.e. "All men are alike." or "Never trust a woman.")

Would you name your daughter after that girl in school you hated? No? Why not? Most likely, you have a negative association with that name. What emotional feelings emerge? When you think of her, you may find there are physical changes in your body such as a flushed face and tensed muscles. Thinking of her will take you to that particular memory basin and you will probably relive the sensory experiences and emotional feelings you felt during an encounter with her. Your brain chemistry changes accordingly.

Memories are not stored with exact data like you might see on videotape. Anything that happens to us goes through our own unique filter first, and is experienced and recorded according to our perceptions and subjective experiences. Our developmental stage at the time a memory first occurs significantly affects what is stored in our memory basins. If you are experiencing something as a three year old, it will be experienced and stored through the eyes of a three year old. You are obviously not going to have the same cognitive abilities at age three that you will have at age thirty-three.

I'll give you a perfect, but embarrassing example. When I was about five years old my family took one of our many trips to Tennessee to visit relatives. I left behind my little goldfish in his tiny round bowl sitting on a corner shelf in our living room. When I returned my goldfish and his bowl were missing. My parents told me that a burglar came in and stole my goldfish while I was away. I trusted and believed them. I was upset, but eventually forgot about it — until I was about forty years old.

I was sharing some family photographs with friends and family and ran across a picture taken before the goldfish theft. There was my beloved goldfish, content in his bowl. I started telling them how my goldfish was stolen when it suddenly occurred to me that my fish died and my parents lied to protect me. They may not have been comfortable trying to explain death to a five year old, or maybe they thought I would be mad at them for KILLING my goldfish. (I'll get over it eventually.) After my realization, I felt incredibly stupid and everyone had a good laugh.

My memories of the incident were well preserved from my five year old perspective. I never questioned the accuracy. It was only looking back on it from my forty year old perspective that I saw what happened. You can "re-call" (call into the present) any conscious memory complete with the sensory input and emotional feelings, *as it was recorded*, including any inaccuracies that may have existed at the time. You can also have physical (body) memories and not remember the context from which they came.

I didn't know why I had such a strong negative response to honey, or anything with honey in it, until I mentioned it to my mother one day. She said that when I was about five years old she bought some honey when we were on a trip to Tennessee. Honey, complete with honeycomb, was sold at roadside stands along the way and still is. When we got home I asked her how you eat it and she replied, "With a spoon." When she wasn't looking, I took a spoon and ate nearly the whole jar of honey. I became very nauseous and never wanted honey again, even though I don't remember ever eating it. My body still responds with the same body memories of feeling ill just at the sight of honey. All of the sensory and emotional experiences are still there, but with no conscious memory of the original encounter with honey.

We can experience body memories without a conscious awareness of the complete memory. This is common in trauma memories where all or parts of the memory are blocked because the experience was too emotionally or physically painful. It is also common in non-trauma memories. We will address more on how memories are stored and retrieved as we get into the techniques of accessing PMOs and developing your other

Super Powers.

Many people don't want to enter therapy for past traumas because they believe they can't change it, so why go through all the pain again? You can't change the past, but you can change how you look at it and experience it today. You can reexamine old traumas or painful experiences through adult eyes and with adult cognitive abilities. You can gain insight and perspective that can change how you presently experience that trauma and heal. There is scientific evidence that words can heal. Dr. Baxter Lewis, psychiatrist at UCLA, has proven that words that are meaningful to someone can activate the same areas of the brain as prescribed drugs such as Prozac (11).

We all change our brain chemistry moment by moment whether we are consciously aware of it or not. Your thoughts change your brain chemistry. Think of a past experience when you felt incredibly sad. Remember it in as much sensory detail as you can. Give yourself a moment to feel the full impact of your feelings. You just changed your brain chemistry.

We feel a full range of emotions when we read a book or watch a movie even though we know it isn't real. We experience it as though it is real, and identify with the characters. We may choose a movie based on our mood and what type of emotional experience we want. It can be upsetting to get surprised with disturbing emotions if you thought you were going to see something lighter.

Have you ever seen a horror movie in 3-D? Several years ago, my kids talked me into seeing *Friday the Thirteenth 3-D*. They loved it. It was too intense and scary for me. The flight or fight chemicals released when we feel afraid or threatened were surging through my brain and I had to take the glasses off or flee.

What is the scariest thing that ever happened to you? What is the scariest movie you've ever seen? You can go to that memory basin simply by thinking about it and your brain chemistry will change accordingly. Now, think of the person or persons you love most in the world. How do you feel when you think of them? A genuine smile on your face indicates a dopamine release. You just accessed the pleasure systems of your brain. *You already know how to access PMOs. You just don't know you know yet.*

We are motivated by the need or desire to feel good, or at least feel better. Consider how addictions are manifested. How many times have you heard someone say they want to quit smoking but smoking helps them with stress so they continue to smoke. Do you know someone who compulsively eats when they are sad or bored? How many relationships break up because the "feeling" just isn't there anymore? Accessing PMOs gives you a natural way to feel good without substances and can breathe new life into stale relationships. Accessing PMOs puts you in control of you, not a substance or another person.

Challenging Your Limiting Beliefs

Our belief system affects everything we think, feel and do. Beliefs are incredibly powerful. Robert Ader, Psychologist, Rochester New York, conducted a taste-aversion experiment with rats conditioning them to dislike the taste of a sweetener when it was given with a drug that caused a stomachache. The researchers didn't know at the time that the drug also caused damage to the immune system.

After the drug/sweetener association was made, the drug was withdrawn, but the rats were still given the sweetened water. Some of them died because every time they drank the sweetened water they *believed* they were getting the drug even though they were not, and their bodies responded accordingly, weakening their immune systems and killing them (8). This belief factor is how the placebo effect works.

We each develop our own unique map or view of the world

based on our experiences and how we process them. This is referred to in NLP as "mapping." We are influenced by our culture, society, family, heredity, environment and our life experiences. Everything we experience is filtered through our belief system. We develop our personal values, interests, assumptions and beliefs based on how we process these experiences. Our interpretations of our experiences influences the filter that each new experience goes through and, thus, affects our thinking and behavior.

If a child grows up being physically and/or sexually abused it is likely that child will develop a belief that the world is a hostile, unsafe place and people cannot be trusted. How many other life experiences would or could be affected by that filter or belief?

What about intimacy in a romantic relationship? Would a person with this filter be predominantly attracted to those who would prove their belief to be true? Would everyone else be filtered out? What we believe to be true, we experience as true. Luckily for us, our filters can change as we seek to change them.

To further explore the power of beliefs, let's think about a time you believed something negative was true and later found it wasn't. Have you ever believed (with certainty) that someone you trusted betrayed you and accused them of it? How did you feel inside when you believed it was true? I imagine it was very emotionally painful. Your body, your mind and your soul reacted as though it were a fact, because you believed it was real.

How did you feel when you found out you were wrong? Maybe you felt foolish and remorseful. You experienced all that worry and pain for nothing. You experienced it as real because you believed it was real.

The same principle can work in reverse. You don't believe something that is true. Sometimes this is a simple misunderstanding or sometimes it is denial. We all experience denial. It is our built in protection from psychological pain. It can have a useful purpose or it can be very detrimental, depending on the circumstances.

Have you ever been on the receiving end, where someone accused you of something you didn't do but they believed it was true? That is a frustrating place to be. Sometimes you can never convince someone that you are innocent no matter what the truth is. Our beliefs have great impact on our lives. They guide and direct us and help us make major life decisions, for better or worse.

The power of beliefs is a key component of NLP. Negative beliefs are referred to in NLP as limiting beliefs. We all have them. As young children we grow up believing what we are told about ourselves, or what we assume to be true based on others' reactions and responses to us.

You can change your limiting beliefs and a whole new world can open up for you, unless, of course, you don't believe you can. Do you believe you can't lose weight? Do you believe you are not smart enough for the career you'd like to have? Do you believe you can't overcome a fear or phobia? Do you believe you can have only one orgasm per sexual experience, if you are lucky?

What if I told you that scientific research shows that women have the capability of having *limitless* orgasms restricted only by fatigue (13)? What is your Maximum Orgasmic Potential (MOP)? Don't be surprised if you don't know. Don't be surprised if you've never even questioned it. It is very much tied into your belief system. You may be limiting your potential by what you believe to be true or untrue.

Women can have one orgasm after another and only be limited by exhaustion. If you didn't know this though, you would not have the expectation of it happening, much less know how to make it happen easily. Accessing PMOs helps you learn more about your own body and learn how to experience the maximum pleasure in a sexual relationship.

Your ability to access PMOs also helps your partner experience maximum pleasure. Men are typically more excited by visual sexual stimulation. Seeing his partner so turned on can be a turn on, especially if he believes he is responsible. It can eliminate performance anxiety, unleash inhibitions and maximize intensity for both partners.

The continuous pulsating muscle contractions that happen during female multiple orgasms can be very stimulating for a man during intercourse. A woman's vaginal muscle strength can increase dramatically with all that automatic and effortless exercise. Women can develop control over their vaginal muscles.

It is unlikely the average person experiences their MOP on a regular basis. PMOs can give you that experience. Since a woman is only limited by fatigue, how does that translate into MOP? For the sake of my poor math skills (limiting belief), let's say that the average female orgasm lasts about 10 seconds. Let us further say that the average sexual experience from beginning to end lasts about 30 minutes. There are 60 seconds in a minute. You do the math.

Am I saying that women can have multiple orgasms throughout a sexual experience, so many that it would be impossible to count? Yes, I am definitely saying that! With PMOs, women can have orgasms at the slightest touch, caress and kiss, or by simply telling themselves to, with no contact at all. Women can teach themselves to have a "hair trigger," if you will. Men and women can learn to increase the intensity of the orgasms, and extend the length of time the orgasms are experienced.

In the next chapter, you will learn how to design and set your own personal PMOs "remote control", which of course can be reset as your skills increase.

If you are one of the many women who have limiting beliefs about your orgasmic potential, then the place to start is to explore and challenge those beliefs. The following assessment questionnaire is designed for women to assess their limiting beliefs and explore their orgasmic potentials. Men can also use the questionnaire to explore their limiting beliefs regarding sexuality and sexual prowess.

Assessing Your Limiting Beliefs Regarding Your Sexuality

1. My most positive sexual experience was:

2. My most negative sexual experience was:

3. My views on sex were influenced by:

4. I think sex is:

5. My partner thinks sex is:

6. My mother thought sex was:

7. My father thought sex was:

8. A good girl/boy is:

9. A bad girl/boy is:

10. What I dislike most about my body is:

11. What I like most about my body is:

12. When I look into the mirror I see:

13. What I would like to see in the mirror is:

14. If I were more attractive or sexy, I am afraid that:

15. I feel sexually inhibited or uncomfortable in the following situations:

    Feelings that arise at these times are:

    I feel that way because:

    I would feel more comfortable if:

16. Sexual acts my partner likes or requests that I am uncomfortable with include:

    Feelings that arise at these times are:

    I feel that way because:

I would feel more comfortable if:

17. During a sexual experience, I feel most embarrassed or ashamed when:

18. The most orgasms I have had during one sexual experience is:

19. The highest number of orgasms I expect to achieve during one sexual experience is:

20. I can have multiple orgasms under the following conditions:

21. If I woke up tomorrow and I (or my partner) could have multiple orgasms any time I (he/she) choose for as long as I (he/she) wanted, the changes in my live would include:

After you complete the questionnaire and you have explored the many influences that have made this a truth for you, take a moment to process your thoughts and feelings. Did any of your answers surprise you?

Sometimes people feel they want to change in a particular area, but not changing can have a secondary gain or type of payoff. I recall a previous client who wanted to lose weight. She struggled with a weight problem most of her life. During treatment she discovered she was afraid to lose weight because she believed she would become promiscuous if she were thinner and more attractive.

She connected these feelings to childhood sexual abuse by her father. She believed she was bad and felt a great deal of shame and guilt over something she didn't do. He committed a shameful and criminal act. She was a small and innocent child. Children are also sexual beings. Sexual touch can feel good to a child. She was filled with self-loathing for wanting her father's touch. Sexual touch was the only type of touch he ever gave her. Her weight served a purpose, but it came with a "heavy" price tag.

Reaching your MOP and learning to use PMOs in and of itself will not make you promiscuous. It can return (or help keep) a romantic relationship to the "in love" stage indefinitely. PMOs can be used in whatever way you choose to use them, including weight loss, decreasing pain, anxiety and depression. Accessing PMOs can enhance your monogamous relationship to such a degree you may find yourself very happy right where you are.

Changing Limiting Beliefs

If you have a limiting belief that you would like to change, here are some steps to move you in that direction.

1. **Define your limiting belief and in what context it occurs.** For example, if you believe you are less valuable as a person than most people you know (low self-esteem), when do you feel this way (i.e. if someone comes over and your house isn't clean, when you have a negative balance in your checking account, and so on)?

2. **Explore what you are doing that maintains your limiting belief.** In *Introducing NLP*, by Joseph O'Connor and John Seymour, the question is posed, "What does the person have to keep doing to maintain the problem?"

Using the above examples, are you fueling your limiting belief when you let your housework go or don't keep track of expenditures? Could you be subconsciously keeping this limiting belief alive by continually reinforcing it?

3. **Notice the self-talk ("old tapes") you use that reinforces your limiting belief and reword in the positive.** What messages have you received throughout your life that has shaped your limiting belief? Are any of these messages from people you love and trust? Turn each negative message into a positive one. Play the positive messages like a broken record and challenge the limiting belief each time it appears. Limiting beliefs usually develop over time, so it takes time to replace them with empowering beliefs.

4. **Observe present messages you are receiving from others and set healthy boundaries.** If you find you have relationships that reinforce your negative belief, set boundaries that do not permit the negative messages to continue. For example, if you're talking to your mother on the phone and she makes a comment that gives you a "you are less than" message, either let her know how you feel and that you don't appreciate that, or if you aren't ready to be confrontive, end the conversation.

5. **Imagine what life will be like when your limiting belief is changed.** Project into the future and imagine life over the next one, five and ten years if your limiting belief stays the same. Now imagine life without it. What will be different? Visualize how your daily experiences will be different after you have released your limiting belief and it is no longer a truth for you. What opportuni-

ties are now available to you?

6. **Fake it until you make it and *give yourself permission to release your limiting belief.*** No matter how strongly you believe your limiting belief now, pretend you don't believe it and act accordingly. Give yourself permission to let your limiting belief go, and live life as it was intended for you.

If, after exploring a limiting belief, you decide to keep that belief for whatever reason, then know it is okay to accept that part of you. Accept the limitations you choose to keep, but recognize it as the choice it is. This can be very freeing. Self-acceptance is an important part of assessing limiting beliefs. Very often the negative or limiting part of a belief can also serve a positive purpose, depending on your perspective.

Our brains are intricate and complex inner galaxies filled with strengths and powers beyond our present comprehension. We are only beginning to understand how to use them. Accessing PMOs is just one example of harnessing this energy and utilizing an ability that has been sleeping. Your ability to draw upon your own personal strengths and abilities, your Super Powers, has absolutely everything to do with what you believe. It is said the body cannot achieve what the mind cannot conceive. So drop the barriers and conceive, believe and then achieve!

DEVELOPING YOUR SUPER POWERS

Chapter Three

TECHNIQUES FOR PHYSICAL MEMORY ORGASMS

*If you want to succeed you should
strike out on new paths,
rather than travel the worn
paths of accepted success.*

John D. Rockefeller, Sr.

Steps to Access PMOs

The information in Chapters 1 and 2 provides the foundation for accessing PMOs and developing your other Super Powers. Hormone balance is of crucial importance if you are experiencing a low sex drive or inability to have orgasms. We have explored options for both men and women who are having difficulty in this area.

You have been introduced to some of the NLP techniques that relate to accessing PMOs, and you will learn more about these techniques in detail. We have delved into the importance of personal beliefs and any limiting beliefs you may have pertaining to your views on sex and your sexuality. You have also learned the significance of exploring your Maximum Orgasmic Potential.

You will learn how to develop a self-awareness that brings more of your experiences from your subconscious into a higher level of consciousness. This self-awareness not only allows you to tap into your ability to access PMOs, but develop your many other Super Powers as well. Here are the steps to accessing PMOs:

Step 1. Explore your Maximum Orgasmic Potential (MOP)

In the learning phase, physical exploration is an essential building block to accessing PMOs. We all have different comfort levels regarding self-touch. If you are uncomfortable touching your own body, you may be even more interested in accessing PMOs because you can experience ecstasy without any touch.

How you use physical self-exploration is up to you. The purpose or goal is to identify your Maximum Orgasmic Potential (MOP) and increase your Maximum Orgasmic Experience (MOE). To put it simply, how far can you go (MOP) and how far have you been so far (MOE) in terms of number of orgasms during one sexual encounter.

On the questionnaire in Chapter 2, you were asked "The most orgasms I have had during one sexual experience is?" Unless that number has changed since you answered the question originally, then that is your *current* maximum orgasmic experience. Your MOE can increase at any time. The term Maximum Orgasmic Potential could be considered a misnomer if you are female, since a woman's orgasmic potential is unlimited.

Learn at your own pace. Become comfortable with your body. This might include something like not wearing underwear at bedtime (or other times), looking at yourself in the mirror after a shower/bath, or taking a little longer putting on your clothes.

If you are a person who is uncomfortable exploring your own

body, you can explore your orgasmic potential with your partner, or you could chose a form of stimulation that doesn't require touching. It doesn't matter how you do it. In whatever way you are comfortable, or that you find acceptable, discover your Maximum Orgasmic Potential, and work on increasing your Maximum Orgasmic Experience.

Learning to access PMOs is a type of retraining your body and mind to experience many intense orgasms and to start it will initially mean some form of physical stimulation. You are teaching yourself to experience multiple orgasms. If you already experience multiple orgasms you may be a step ahead. Expanding your MOE will test what might be your own self-imposed limits.

Challenge yourself to see how far you can go. It is okay to let your body do what it was designed to do. Some may believe the female's ability to experience unlimited multiple orgasms is compensation for the other physical adversities women go through, like menstruation and the physical pain of childbirth.

The more you experience orgasm the easier it becomes. Your orgasm basin (memory) will be deepening. You may also experience orgasms in your sleep during this phase of learning and sexual desire will likely increase.

With short-term memory, a neuron's electrical signal stays charged for days or possibly weeks. With long-term memory, the electrical traces are transferred into physical chemical traces called substrates, or memory engrams. Research has shown that at least some memories physically exist in our brains. In *The Learning Brain*, Eric Jenson states, "Memory looks like electrical signals with a reduced flow of potassium across a membrane, much like the strokes of a painting."

These memory traces have been identified when classical conditioning is used. When a learned task is repeated over and over again, and there is a reward associated with this task, the neurological connections become stronger. A behavior becomes automatic through repetition.

Think of the neurological wiring that results in orgasm as a baseball diamond in a grassy yard. The more you run the bases, the deeper the path becomes, and the easier it is to get to home base. The repeated behavior that results in an established electrical pathway not only becomes easier to access, it can happen faster, like having a service that gives you quicker access to the Net. You don't have to wait as long to get where you want to go.

This is why developing your MOP is such an important step in learning to access PMOs. If you find some limiting beliefs getting in your way, go back to that chapter and do more exploring.

For some men it may not be desirable to get to home base faster. However, if you have difficulty with orgasm or sexual arousal, you may be interested in these particular techniques to become sexually aroused quickly.

Summary - Step 1: Explore your Maximum Orgasmic Potential (MOP). How many orgasms can you have during one sexual experience (with a partner or solo): Deepen this neurological pathway by having as many orgasms as you can during each sexual experience, and continue to challenge yourself.

Step 2. Bring Your Orgasmic Experience Into Your Conscious Awareness

The next step in accessing PMOs is learning how to bring into your conscious awareness what you do subconsciously during orgasm. Imagine if you were required to write a six-page report on your breathing patterns throughout your workday as a part of a productivity study. Your level of consciousness would have to shift to complete this task. The same is true when you are learning to access PMOs.

As you explore your MOP, pay very close attention to how-this feels physically throughout your *body* and in your *head.* What sensations do you feel in your head just before you have an orgasm? Generally, you know when it is about to begin. What tells you? What sensations do you feel throughout your body just before you have an orgasm? Make a mental inventory and *memorize* it. You may be concerned that self-observation will interfere with your pleasure. Ultimately, this greater awareness will dramatically increase your pleasure. Once you learn how to access PMOs, you don't have to use this type of concentration. It becomes effortless.

This keen observation brings into your consciousness the processes your body naturally goes through during orgasm. Once you have this awareness, you can trigger orgasms by giving yourself the mental command to do so, just as you tell yourself to do anything. Every inch of the body is mapped in an organized manner in the brain and can be activated with thought (10, 16).

If you were driving somewhere you have never been before and had to remember how to get back, you might find yourself paying attention to details you would otherwise never notice. *Use whatever mental strategy works for you, but the goal is to know and remember precisely what happens in your head and throughout your body before, during and after orgasm.*

Summary – Step 2: Bring the mental and physical processes you experience just *before* and *during* orgasm into your conscious awareness through self-observation. What is happening in your head and your body? Pay attention to your experiences and commit them to memory.

Step 3. Practice Recalling the Mental and Physical Processes Experienced During Orgasm

Once you feel you have these mind and body sensations committed to memory, practice *recalling* the sensations you experience just *before* orgasm *without* using any physical stimulation at all. Simply think about these physical feelings. Bring them to mind by remembering what they are.

You may get sexually aroused reading a romantic novel, seeing your favorite star on the screen, or thinking of someone you find sexually attractive. You already know how to activate these pleasure systems in your head.

If you have difficulty, go ahead and use whatever physical stimulation is necessary to bring yourself to the point of *almost* having an orgasm and then stop. Without touch, practice recalling those sensations again. If you can have an orgasm without touch at this point, then, by all means go ahead. Either way, continue with the other techniques and practice, practice, practice. As with learning any new skill, practice makes perfect.

Summary – Step 3: Without any stimulation, recall the mental and physical sensations you feel just *before* and *during* orgasm and experience them in the present. If you have difficulty recalling these sensations, use physical stimulation initially. Repetition is the secret to success.

Step 4. Identify and Memorize Your Physical Positioning and Physical Signals for Orgasm

There are many physical changes that occur when we experience orgasm. Of course, the physical changes a man experiences during orgasm are different than those a woman experiences. Even so, we do share common ground.

There are four distinct phases in the female sexual response cycle. These phases are the excitement, plateau, orgasm and resolution phases. In the excitement or arousal phase, some of the physical changes that occur includes: vaginal lubrication, increase in size of the clitoris, labia and nipples, expansion of the vagina and the upward pulling of the uterus and cervix.

During the plateau phase a woman may feel an increase in

sexual tension, the outer one-third of the vagina may swell, decreasing the size of the opening, the inner two-thirds of the vagina expands like a partially blown up balloon. Also, there is a tightening of the muscles in the thighs and buttocks.

During the orgasmic phase, muscle contractions occur in the other one-third of the vagina, the uterus and the anus. These contractions are just under one second apart. The number of contractions, and, therefore, the length of the orgasm can vary. Most or all of your body muscles contract or tighten during orgasm. This can make PMOs a highly rewarding and effortless way to exercise.

The pubococcygus (PC) muscle plays a significant role in accessing PMOs. Strengthening the PC muscle intensifies orgasm in both men and women. In both sexes, the urethra and rectum pass through this muscle. Multiple orgasms strengthens the PC muscle as well as many other muscles, including tightening the muscles of the vagina and giving you more control in this area.

On another interesting note, nearly all women curl their toes during orgasm and their nipples become erect. There are other physical changes, but we're looking at only those that may be relevant to accessing PMOs.

During the resolution phase, a woman can continue to experience orgasms by moving back and forth between the plateau phase and the orgasm phase. Usually, the closer together they are, the easier it is to keep going. Once she feels ready to stop, her body will return to the pre-excitement or resolution phase.

Men have the same basic four phases, with the addition of a refractory period after orgasm. This is the time in between erections. The refractory period may lengthen as a man becomes older.

During the male excitement phase, the brain releases nitric oxide that dilates the vessels that supply blood to the penis resulting in an erection. During this phase the brain will spew out natural endorphins. The longer the excitement phase continues, the more intense the man's orgasm will be. The phase between excitement and orgasm is the equivalent to the female plateau phase.

An orgasm is an involuntary process consisting of muscle contractions and release of sexual tension. Blood pressure and heart rate increases. The sensation of the build up of seminal fluid lets a man know he is nearing orgasm. The testicles move up closer to his body. The urinary tract to the bladder closes, and the muscular contractions of orgasm start.

The number of contractions and length of time of the orgasm is about the same as it is with women. The muscle contractions occur at the base of the penis, the penis shaft, around the anal sphincter, rectum and the PC muscle. It is these contractions that give a man the euphoric sensations he feels during orgasm, not the actual ejaculation.

Learning the techniques used to access PMOs could help a man more easily move into the excitement phase, extend the plateau stage, and enhance and lengthen the orgasm phase.

I'd like to pose an interesting question. Since it is the muscle contractions that give the sensations felt during orgasm, can a man learn to recall those sensations (physical memories) and trigger this in his brain without the full experience of orgasm with ejaculation, resulting in multiple orgasms for men? Since women can recall just the trigger of orgasm that results in these muscle contractions with no physical or mental stimulation, can men do the same?

Whether you are male or female, identify the signals and physical indicators of impending orgasm and orgasm then commit them to memory. As you observe yourself in these four phases of sexual arousal, pay very close attention to what you do physically with your body. For instance, if you are a woman, you may feel an expanding or tenting in your vagina, or you may push down with your vaginal muscles.

Techniques For Physical Memory Orgasms

There is a particular triggering of the release of orgasm that you can identify once you become more consciously aware of your experience. This triggering signals the brain to release those pleasure chemicals. Your trigger(s) may be a particular way you position or move your body just before orgasm, such as tightening your PC muscle. It may take a few seconds for that signal to travel to your brain and the orgasms begin. Once you have identified the signal that triggers orgasm, you can activate it by recalling it with thought, or you can trigger it by a body movement you have identified as a physical trigger. It is important that you identify *your* triggers. Don't try to follow someone else's guide.

Observing closely each and every physical movement you make before, during and after orgasm can be the quickest and easiest route to accessing PMOs. Going through the simple physical motions you experience during orgasm can trigger orgasm. As you continue to explore your MOP and become more skilled with accessing PMOs, this neurological pathway will be deepened. Once your path is worn, don't let any grass grow under your feet!

Our thoughts direct our mind, body and actions from moment to moment. You know how to do many things with your body, most of which you don't give much thought. Some easily recognizable examples are burping, passing gas, yawning, urinating, blowing your nose and sniffing. Each one of these body functions requires a particular physical movement or action that you know how to do and can trigger with thought if you want to.

Once you pay attention to and remember how you have orgasms, you can trigger orgasms with thought just as you do any other body function. You can remember the physical experience of orgasm or sexual arousal, including the sensations in your head as your brain chemistry changes and pleasure chemicals are released, and bring it into the present, at will.

You do not have to go through the excitement or plateau phases of the sexual response cycle. It takes no mental or physical preparation, such as sexual fantasy or sexual stimulation. You can have multiple orgasms instantly and not have a single sexual thought or feeling in your mind or body. If you want to release those natural pleasure chemicals in your brain, for whatever the purpose, you can do it by simply deciding to.

Summary – Step 4: Pay attention to your body positioning and the physical movements you make just before and during orgasm. You will discover that there are particular triggers that happen just before orgasm that signal your brain to release your natural pleasure chemicals. You may find this is as simple as tightening your PC muscle, but each individual will have his/her own physical positioning and signals. You will learn your positioning and signals through the self-observation in Step 2.

Step 5. Associate the Mental and Physical Sensations You Feel During Orgasm with Anchors

Another NLP technique that is the crux of PMOs is called anchoring. An anchor is a stimulus that triggers a response. Joseph O'Connor and John Seymour state in *Introducing NLP*, "An anchor is anything that accesses an emotional state." Anchors work through association. There are countless examples of anchors we use every day. There are anchors that are generally uniformly recognized. A red light is a visual anchor that signals us to stop. An alarm clock is an auditory anchor that tells us when to get up. Some anchors are individual. The smell of cigarette smoke may trigger a smoker to want a cigarette. The same smell would probably trigger a nonsmoker to get away from the smoke. There are also tangible anchors. A baseball player may have a lucky hat, or football player may have a lucky jersey.

Anchors work through classical conditioning. The Russian scientist, Ivan Pavlov, is famous for his experiments with dogs that salivated when they heard a bell. The dogs learned to associate the ringing of the bell with getting food and salivated when they heard the bell, whether food was present or not. The bell was an auditory anchor (stimulus) that triggered a conditioned (learned) response (salivating) in anticipation of food. What type of brain chemistry changes do you experience when you see your favorite food on TV? The marketing and advertising industries are well aware of association, classical conditioning and the power of suggestion.

Classical conditioning is a part of almost everything we do What is money? Isn't it just distinct looking pieces of paper? The paper itself isn't worth anything, but what it represents keeps us working every day. Association is essential for storing memory and being able to retrieve it at a later time.

In an article titled *Placebo Effect: The Power of the Sugar Pill*, Julio Rocha do Amarai, M.D. and Renato M.E. Sabbatini, Ph.D., describe a scientific experiment designed to test the placebo effect.

A dog was given an injection of acetylcholine (neurotransmitter) after hearing a sound stimulus (alarm ringing). This injection lowered the dog's blood pressure. This was done several times. Then the dog was given an injection of adrenaline instead of acetylcholine, after hearing the alarm.

Adrenaline would typically increase the dog's blood pressure but, because of the conditioned response to the alarm sound, the dog's blood pressure continued to lower. The conditioned response of the lower blood pressure was engraved (baseball path) in the dog's central nervous system and that learned response overrode the potential effects of the adrenaline.

There can be more than one stimulus (anchor) to get the same response. In the above-noted experiment, the alarm acted as an anchor. However, the act of injection, the needle used for the injections, and the person giving the injections are all anchors that trigger the lowered blood pressure response, if the dog learns to make these associations.

Developing anchors to access PMOs can be done easily. An anchor works like using your password to access the Internet. You "type" it in and go where you want to go. Once you have identified what feeling you experience in your head just before and during orgasm, and what physical movements trigger orgasm, associate it with a physical anchor to help you recall it and re-experience it in the present.

This physical anchor can be as simple as touching your index finger to your thumb, or slightly curling the end of your tongue with your mouth closed. You will probably want your anchor to be something inconspicuous, for obvious reasons. The body positioning you identified as physical signals just before or during orgasm can be used as an anchor, such as curling your toes or slightly digging in with your nails. Once you have chosen your physical anchor, do it every time you are having an orgasm. Which physical anchor you choose isn't as important as the association you make with it.

When you use an anchor you are conditioning (teaching) yourself to have a learned response of orgasm and associating orgasm with the anchor. When you access PMOs, a flood of natural pleasure chemicals are released, reinforcing this learned behavior.

Just because the learned response is orgasm doesn't have to mean you are looking for sexual gratification. You are triggering a release of pleasure brain chemicals that have multiple benefits. Endorphins and dopamine reduce anxiety and depression, and endorphins naturally reduce pain. A nice dopamine release gets you moving and motivated. PEA decreases appetite, gives you energy and makes you feel happy and more connected to your partner. These pleasure brain chemicals are the lead ingredients to the brain chemistry "cocktail" of orgasm, but they are also present in varying amounts with any pleasant state of mind.

You can also make a partner or specific acts with your partner a physical anchor. You can experience multiple orgasms simply by kissing or touching your partner, if you choose these acts as a physical anchor. Any particular physical trait your partner has can be used as an anchor. That could be looking into his/her eyes (visual anchor), touching his/her hair (touch anchor) or whatever you choose it to be.

Maybe you saw the *Seinfeld* episode where George inadvertently began associating food with sexual arousal. Food acted as his anchor. The shampoo commercial that shows a woman having an "orgasmic" experience when she uses their organic shampoo is an example of associating an anchor (the shampoo) with orgasm. If you chose that particular brand of shampoo as an anchor, what is implied in that commercial could be real. Of course, you can use any brand of shampoo or anything else you choose as an anchor to access PMOs. Avoid using too many anchors at first. Become proficient with two or three and then gradually add more.

You are making an association between your anchor(s) and orgasm, or sexual arousal. Once you have decided which anchors you wish to use to access PMOs, use the same anchor(s) consistently for the learned response you want. In NLP this learned response is referred to as a desired state of mind.

Using anchors for desired states of mind can be used for any desired state you wish. You can anchor a desired state when you are presently in it and recall it later, and/or recall past times when you were in this desired state and anchor it. Any human state of mind can be accessed when you want or need it. With more practice, you will find that thought alone will access a desired state, including PMOs. You will learn to choose your state of mind, and change your brain chemistry at will.

Summary – Step 5: Associate the mental and physical sensations you feel during orgasm/sexual arousal with anchors (a stimulus that triggers a response). This is classical conditioning. You can associate a verbal, physical or tangible anchor with orgasm/sexual arousal. A verbal anchor would be a word you say aloud or to yourself. A physical anchor would be something you do physically with your body, like curling your toes, or touching your index finger to your thumb. A tangible anchor is something you can touch, such as your partner or any part of him/her, thereof. Anchors are used to trigger PMOs.

Step 6. Categorize and Name Your Orgasmic Experiences

As you continue to reach your MOP, you will probably find that orgasms are not all the same in sensation and degree of intensity. The next step in learning to access PMOs is categorizing and naming your orgasms.

Some sexologists categorize female orgasms as clitoral orgasms, vaginal orgasms and/or uterine orgasms (whatever that is). Some women have difficulty having an orgasm during intercourse, but can have an orgasm with stimulation of the clitoris. Women without uteruses will have to rule out uterine orgasms. You may be interested to know that the clitoris is actually about nine inches long. Only the tip can be seen. The rest is inside the body in a wishbone shape branching out on each side of the vagina.

The type of categorizing and naming of orgasms used to access PMOs is more detailed and specific than the three listed above. Categorizing and naming orgasms provides you with verbal anchors and exact physical memories to recall your orgasms.

As you become skilled at bringing into your conscious

Techniques For Physical Memory Orgasms

awareness what happens in your body and mind during sexual arousal and orgasm, it is important to recognize the various types of orgasms you may experience. How do orgasms from water pressure differ from orgasms from intercourse, or orgasms from oral stimulation differ from touching? How does the first orgasm vary from the third or the thirtieth? Does it vary?

Keeping a log or journal of your orgasmic journey can be helpful. Men's orgasmic experiences also vary. If a man wants to experience a stronger, more intense orgasm, he can use these same techniques to anchor his intense orgasms and recall them just before and during orgasm.

The following is for **example only**. It is important that you develop your own unique list because no one can feel your orgasms but you, and you can't recall someone else's experience.

1. **Sweets** — Light and delicious. Feels like little butterfly wings tickling you inside and your head seems to float away. Waves wash over you like the tide ebbing and flowing.

2. **Deep** — Strong, hard contractions and no sense of control. You may feel a strong bonding with your partner.

3. **C's** — Sensation of oral contact. Every nerve ending alive, an electric current moves through you over and over again. All time and space is suspended.

4. **Volcano** — A combination of sweets, C's and Deep. You think your brain will explode and you leave the orbit for a while, very powerful and erupting. This can happen when you combine your anchors for each orgasm and use them one after another. This is referred to in NLP as chaining anchors.

5. **Top Floor** — The highest level you experience — whatever that is for you. You know it when you are there. After practicing PMOs over a period of time, you may find your body does some adjusting and develops a climax of the climaxes. This may be a tremendous head rush accompanied by many rapid firing muscle contactions where you are forced to stop because it is too intense.

6. **Spool Orgasms** — Another type of orgasm that can lead to the Top Floor is something I have dubbed Spool Orgasms. Spool orgasms can happen when you have experienced a great deal of stimulation quickly and the multiple orgasms build. The orgasms have been triggered, but haven't had time to happen and your body has to catch up. When the stimulation stops the orgasms follow in rapid firing succession and may result in the climax of the climaxes. The term "spool" comes from computer language (so I am told). If you hit the print button six times, it takes time for the printer to catch up and produce the order.

7. **Floating** — The feeling of after-glow. A happy, content all-is-right-with-the-world feeling. You can have this feeling anytime, with or without orgasm, whether male or female. Identify how this feels in your head, anchor it, and you can recall just this feeling (desired state) when you want. It can work well to release enough endorphins to take away the pain,, or enough dopamine to improve your moods.

When you choose a verbal and physical anchor for the climax of the climaxes orgasm, it is important not to use it unless your situation permits total abandonment. If it is used when you cannot express it freely, it may dilute the response and not be as effective. You may want to use this anchor less frequently so as not to become habituated to it, and possibly result in the response becoming less intense.

The brain is wired for organization and balance. It will self-adjust and reorganize if something changes in its present organization. If your mind and body are familiar with having one or two orgasms a week and that shifts to multiple orgasms daily, then that becomes the norm. Then, when you have a sexual experience with a partner, what might have previously been on a 1-3 orgasm scale can become non-stop orgasms that cumulate to the climax of the climaxes like nothing you have experienced. The brain seems to adjust to these new experiences by basically keeping the same pattern, but on a much higher plane.

It is important that you observe, experience, commit to memory, physically anchor, categorize and name your own orgasms. When you use your physical anchor and mentally use the name you gave that particular orgasmic experience, you can re-experience it.

Summary – Step 6: Categorize and name your various orgasmic experiences. Distinguish the different types of orgasms you experience and give them a verbal anchor (name). When you want to experience that particular type of orgasm again, you can recall it by thinking of the name you have given it.

There you have it, how to access Physical Memory Orgasms. To recap:

Steps to Accessing Physical Memory Orgasms (PMOs)

1. **Explore your Maximum Orgasmic Potential (MOP).** How many orgasms can you have during one sexual experience (with a partner or solo)? Deepen this neu-

rological pathway by having as many orgasms as you can during each s exual experience, and continue to challenge yourself.

2. Bring the mental and physical processes you experience just *before* and *during* orgasm into your conscious awareness through self-observation. What is happening in your head and your body? Pay attention to your experiences and commit them to memory.

3. Without any physical stimulation, recall the mental and physical sensations you feel just *before* and *during* orgasm and experience them in the present. If you have difficulty recalling these sensations, use physical stimulation initially. Repetition is the secret to success.

4. Pay attention to your body positioning and the physical movements you make just before and during orgasm. You will discover that there are particular triggers that happen just before orgasm that signal your brain to release your natural pleasure chemicals. You may find this is as simple as tightening your PC muscle, but each individual will have his/her own physical positioning and signals.
 You will learn your positioning and signals through the self-observation in Step 2.

5. Associate the mental and physical sensations you feel during orgasm/sexual arousal with anchors (a stimulus that triggers a response). This is classical conditioning. You can associate a verbal, physical or tangible anchor with orgasm/sexual arousal (Ch. 3).

A verbal anchor would be a word you say aloud or to yourself. A physical anchor would be something you do physically with your body, like curling your toes, or touching your index finger to your thumb. A tangible anchor is something you can touch, such as your partner or any part of him/her, thereof. Anchors are used to trigger PMOs.

6. Categorize and name your various orgasmic experiences. Distinguish the different types of orgasms you experience and give them a verbal anchor (name). When you want to experience that particular type of orgasm again, you can recall it by thinking of the name you have given it.

Once you have learned to access PMOs, you may find you don't need any type of anchor. You can use your physical trigger(s) or thought alone to experience limitless orgasms instantly and effortlessly. It becomes as easy as giving yourself the mental command to blink your eyes.

Practice Physical Memory Accessing

You can use Physical Memory Accessing to recall any past physical and sensory memories that you would like to experience in the present. The techniques used to access PMOs are the same techniques used in Physical Memory Accessing. Practicing Physical Memory Accessing can sharpen your skills in accessing PMOs.

In Chapter 2 you were introduced to the concept of physical memories with the example of peanut butter sticking to the roof of your mouth. You can make this physical memory more vivid by taking a small amount of peanut butter, or any food of a like texture, and placing it in your mouth for a moment. How does the metal spoon feel compared to the peanut butter? Observe the feel of the peanut butter and pay attention to any physical processes while you hold it there.

Is holding the peanut butter in your mouth a pleasant or unpleasant experience? If it is an enjoyable sensation you will be accessing the pleasure systems of your brain and may have a smile or look of pleasure on your face. If it is unpleasant, your brain will be releasing stress chemicals, like cortisol, and your face will express your distaste.

What is your brain doing? Notice any sensations in your head. As you start to swallow the peanut butter, what are your tongue and lips doing? Give the experience a physical anchor and a name.

Drink some water to wash the peanut butter away, then practice recalling this physical memory without the peanut butter. Use your anchors and reenact the physical movements you used to eat the peanut butter. Practicing will enable you to recall the physical memory just by thinking about it without the use of anchors. You are simply enhancing a skill you already have and becoming consciously aware of your unconscious processes. It works the same with PMOs.

Try the same process with different types of physical experiences. Try touching something cold for a moment. An ice cube will do. Keep your finger on it until you begin to feel the sting of the cold. What is happening in your head and the rest of your body? What are you doing physically with your body? Are you tensing up? Are you tightening your jaw? Again, give this experience an anchor and practice recalling it.

You can practice recalling any physical experience through your awareness of the process, giving it an anchor(s), and concentrating to recall it. Begin to pay attention to your physical experiences. You can practice throughout the day. Bringing your physical experiences into your conscious awareness will go a long way towards developing your Super Powers and accessing

PMOs.

Setting Your PMOs Remote Control

I have never been good at setting anything, even an alarm clock. If it has buttons, I'm in trouble. Your PMOs remote control doesn't have any buttons, however, at least none you can see. Resetting it as your skills progress is not a problem. You can channel the electrical power between your ears and gain more control over your own neurological circuitry. Once what transpires in your body and mind comes into your conscious awareness, you can learn to direct it.

What buttons and features would you like to have on your PMOs remote control? Some are basic, such as, power (on/off), volume and channels. Other buttons may be more specialized, like, pause or mute. Let's take a look at how this could be relevant in accessing PMOs.

We have already discussed the techniques used in accessing PMOs. Once you have mastered these techniques, you have found your power or "on" button. It is equally important to be able to turn it off. To do this you need to decide on an "off" anchor. This "off" anchor could include a physical anchor, such as closing your eyes briefly or swallowing, as well as a verbal anchor, something you say to yourself. It can be anything you decide. Again, it is the association that is important, not the specific anchors. Once you have become more comfortable accessing PMOs, you may just decide to stop and not need an "off" anchor.

A volume button is generally for sound, but for purposes of accessing PMOs can be used to regulate intensity. You could be in a situation where accessing PMOs is okay, but maybe you don't want someone else to know. You can learn to turn down the volume without missing out on the pleasure. All orgasms don't have to result in noticeable sounds or movements. You can even have a mute button and have silent orgasms.

There may be circumstances when you may not want your partner to know just yet, or you want to rid yourself of pain or improve your mood with no sexual intentions.

As you practice your MOP, and categorize and name your different types of orgasms, you will probably experience varying degrees of intensity. You can recall the less intense orgasms by using the anchor(s) you choose for them. When you are in a setting where total abandonment is well and good, you can turn up the volume and make all the noise and movements you want by using the anchor(s) for those types of orgasms.

Have you ever wanted a particularly delicious orgasm to last forever? This pause button can be helpful for men who want to stay in their plateau phase longer, as well as women who want to linger in Nirvana.

Maybe you saw the movie *Being John Malkovich*. The male lead character entered John's body and mind several times. He learned to gain more control each time and maintain that control for longer periods of time. The same concept is used here, only no one is in control except you. Being able to pause this desired state takes practice, but it is easy once you have developed what is referred to as unconscious competence (14).

We learn through both conscious and unconscious learning. According to Dr. Emile Donchin, at the Champaign-Urbana campus of the University of Illinois, 99% of all learning is nonconscious (11). We actually learn faster and better through unconscious learning than conscious learning. Unconscious learning just means that we are picking up things and processing them constantly without realizing it. To develop unconscious competence, there are four stages of learning. We will use learning to access PMOs as an example.

1. Unconscious incompetence. When you don't even know you don't know something. You've never heard of it before. Regarding PMOs, you may not have known they existed, or that you have that potential, before reading this book.

2. Conscious incompetence. You're reading this book, so you know what PMOs are, but have no idea how to do it. You have the new awareness, but not the know-how.

3. Conscious Competence. This is the stage of learning to access PMOs where you have made your discovery of how to do it, but it is new and takes some concerted effort.

4. Unconscious Competence. When you reach this stage of learning, you know how to access PMOs and you have enough experience to make it second nature. You can access PMOs very easily and effortlessly.

Once you have reached the stage of unconscious competence with accessing PMOs, it is a skill that lasts forever. Have you ever driven somewhere with other things on your mind and don't remember any of the lights or turns and suddenly you are there? Autopilot is an example of unconscious competence.

After developing a level of unconscious competence when accessing PMOs, you can experiment with programming your remote control and expanding your skills. This is limited only by your imagination.

If you want to use your pause button while accessing PMOs, you do it by mentally and physically drawing out the time you spend in that particular desired state. If you were learning any new physical skill such as swimming under water or running long distances, how would you sharpen your ability and increase your distance? Your PMOs pause button works the same way.

The more channels you have access to the more variety and choices you have. Your experience learning to access PMOs is uniquely yours. You may experience something in a way no one else ever has. As you become more skilled at accessing PMOs, the more channels you will have available to you. Your channels will include your categories of orgasms and the varying degree of intensity of them. When you get into the next chapter on Virtual Reality Fantasy, you will have cable. What movie channels you choose will be up to you.

Super Power Techniques to Enhance Sex with Your Partner

Most of the techniques discussed to this point are not dependent on gender or sexual orientation, although some are. There's much to learn from individual experiences. The survey at the end of this book is designed so that readers of both genders and different sexual orientations can share their experiences to help others.

If you are a female with a male partner you may want to learn how to have intense, on-going orgasms during sexual intercourse. If you are a male with a female partner, you may *really* enjoy her ability to do this.

Women can access PMOs during sexual intercourse and the body sensations felt during penetration can become a physical anchor that is associated with orgasm. After this link is made, you may find you have to concentrate to *stop* having orgasms during sexual intercourse if the experience becomes too intense.

Once you have anchored the physical memories of sexual intercourse and the orgasms you have as a result, you can recall these exact physical memories and PMOs even if you are alone. The body sensations and positioning that occur during penetration can be anchored to give you access to this experience anytime you choose it. You can practice recalling the physical memories of penetration and feel the same pressures and sensations that you would feel if it were happening in the present. Your orgasms can be the same or better. The more you practice this technique, the easier it will be to have orgasms during sexual intercourse.

Men can use the same techniques, only obviously with different physical memories and positioning. Men will probably want to prolong their plateau phase as long as possible. This may be more difficult to do with the added intensity. If you are male and you want to prolong your plateau phase, follow the steps to PMOs previously outlined. This includes identifying the mind and body sensations you feel just before orgasm. Pay particular attention to the physical sensations you feel in your penis and brain when you know orgasm is nearing.

You will reach a "point of no return" when you could not stop orgasm no matter what you do because it has already been triggered in your brain. The signal has been given and your body has no choice but to follow through with the command.

The brain chemistry you are experiencing at that exact moment is what you want to memorize and learn to recall with thought. Give your trigger of orgasm a physical anchor and name (verbal anchor). What does this triggering of orgasm feel like? Notice the muscle contractions that occur during orgasm and ejaculation. Again, memorize these exact physical mind-body sensations.

You can learn to draw out your orgasmic experience with your remote control techniques. If you come to orgasm before you want to, it doesn't have to mean the sexual experience is over for either one of you. You can linger in this euphoric state longer. If it starts to slip away, recall your trigger to orgasm with the physical and verbal anchors you have associated with this experience.

Since her orgasms are limitless until fatigue, the slightest movement can continue to trigger her orgasms, erection or not.

You can also continue to recall your orgasmic sensations, even if to a lesser degree, *after* orgasm as you continue to trigger her orgasms. Depending on how long your refractory time is before your next erection, you may never have to "leave the area" before you begin again.

For either gender, your partner may like a particular sexual act that you like to avoid. If your reasons for avoidance are not because it is against your value system, or it is harmful or hurtful to you, you can access positive physical memories during this sexual act and find pleasure.

You can start by using an anchor to access a physical memory of an intense orgasmic experience from a sexual act you enjoy very much and use it during the less desirable sexual act. Keep your thoughts and experiences focused on the intense orgasmic experience that you associate with the more pleasurable sexual act. You can make a new positive association with the less desirable act and it can become much more pleasurable to both you and your partner.

A passionate sex life for a couple can strengthen the bond and intimacy between them. Imagine the ripple effects on the rest of your life.

Physical Limitations and Accessing PMOs

There is a wide range of physical limitations that can effect sexual functioning from effects of medication to paralysis. PMOs are orgasms that can be triggered in your head with no physical stimulation at all. How might this ability benefit someone with a physical limitation that prevents full sexual functioning? How can the ability to access PMOs be maximized in a relationship where one partner has limited sexual functioning and the other does not?

If an adult with past sexual experiences has no sexual functioning due to paralysis, or any other physical reason, can these physical memories be accessed and very real orgasms felt in the present? I am looking to the reader survey to add breadth and depth to this area and others.

Reduced sexual functioning can be much like missing a body part. It is common for a person with a missing limb to experience a "phantom" limb. The physical memories of the limb are still there. Phantom limbs can feel severe pain and it can take many years for the mind to no longer feel the missing limb.

If injury or illness is sustained and results in the loss of function in a particular area, the brain will reorganize and rewire to compensate for that loss. The brain can rewire to give the sensation of the missing limb in other nearby brain regions. This rewiring can begin happening within hours after losing a limb Touching a part of the face may feel like touching a missing thumb as the brain compensates for this loss by rerouting the neurological circuitry. This change in neuro-circuitry can be seen on an MRI (16).

Humans share a common brain map in terms of what location in the brain coincides with what body part. As a note of interest, the foot is located in the brain next to the area where the genitalia are represented. This is thought to be a possible explanation for foot fetishes. The nipples are mapped in the brain near the same area as the ears. One man who lost his foot felt his orgasms in his phantom foot (16)! Pleasure mapping is the technique of discovering where these remapped locations are and accessing them to regain your sense of pleasure from touch.

It would be impossible to address all of the many physical limitations that affect sexual functioning in this space. This is an area where I anticipate future groundbreaking developments. Accessing PMOs is a beginning in harnessing and directing our mind power in ways we may have previously thought impossible or just never considered. As these techniques evolve, contributions can be made to science that can help this and future generations.

DEVELOPING YOUR SUPER POWERS

Chapter Four

VIRTUAL REALITY FANTASY

*In the orientation of the creative
you are naturally and easily
able to build momentum.
Every action you take, whether it is
directly successful or not,
adds additional energy to your path.*

*Because of this, everything you do
works towards creating eventual success,
including those things which
are not immediately successful.
Over a period of time, creating the results
you want gets easier and easier.*

Robert Fritz

Virtual Reality Fantasy Techniques

Virtual Reality Fantasy is another Super Power you can add to your repertoire. The difference between fantasy and Virtual Reality Fantasy (VRF) is that VRF is intensified, enhanced imagery that is experienced on a more real level. This is done by breaking down your sensory experiences into detail (submodalities) and viewing the fantasy from different perceptions (perceptual position). Submodalities and perceptual position are techniques used in NLP.

Submodalities are *specific* sensory descriptors using the five senses of sight, sound, touch, taste and smell. A specific sensory descriptor using the sense of sight is whether a mental image is in black and white or color. Choose a current event and "see" it in your mind's eye. Continue to describe the mental image in more detail. Is the image large or small, close or faraway, clear or out of focus? When you give your more detailed description you are using submodalities.

Perceptual position refers to viewing something from 1) first position (your own perception), 2) second position (the other person's perception), or 3) third position (an observer's perception).

Perceptual position basically means whose eyes are you seeing through, whose ears are you hearing from, or whose shoes are you standing in depending on your dominant sense. If you are remembering or imagining a situation from your own experience this is first position. If you are remembering or imagining it from another's perception, this is second position. Third position is experiencing it as an observer, as though it is a scene in a movie and you are in the audience. Having the flexibility to move from the first, second and third position can give you greater versatility.

VRF is using mental imagery, sounds, tastes, smells and feelings that you control, enhance, or change to experience the fantasy more fully. The following are examples of categories of submodalities. Don't limit yourself to this list. There are many more possibilities. Use what best conveys your experience.

<u>Visual</u>
Color/black and white

Bright/dim
Size of the image
Location and distance

Auditory
Volume high/low
Tone — soft//harsh
Clarity
Rate of speech — fast/slow

Kinesthetic (Touch)
Location — where touched
Pressure — hard/soft
Duration
Temperature — external and internal

Olfactory (Smell)
Pleasant/offensive
Intensity — strong/faint

Gustatory (Taste)
Flavorful/foul
Bitter/sweet/salty

It can be helpful to determine your primary learning sense before you begin focusing on the sensory details of your fantasy. A visual learner thinks primarily in pictures. You say it and they see it. The types of phrases you use indicate your more dominant sense. Visual phrases may include, "I see what you mean." Or, "Show me what you mean."

An auditory learner tends to think in sounds and will more easily recall memories by sound than any other sense. When they listen to someone speak, the eyes of an auditory learner will generally move from side to side, as if reading a book.

Auditory learners may need a little longer to process information than a visual learner. Phrases an auditory learner may use include, "That rings a bell." Or, "We are on the same wavelength."

A kinesthetic (touch) or olfactory/gustatory (smell/taste) learner largely thinks in feelings, and could be perceived by some as a bit intrusive because they frequently touch, smell and taste things. Phrases you would hear from a kinesthetic learner include, "I feel it in my gut." Or, "I will get in touch with you." Olfactory and Gustatory Phrases include, "She is a sweet person." Or, "That stinks."

You will probably recognize yourself in more than one example, and, of course, we learn by using all of our senses. Even someone who is visually impaired or blind can have the neurological wiring of a visual learner. Once you identify your preferred sense you can experience your VRFs on a more intense level by focusing on the sensory descriptors that best match your dominant sense first, then move into the descriptors of your other four senses. Recognizing your partner's dominant sense can also be a plus whether your communication is sensual or you are in an argument. Understanding that each individual has different ways of processing information can improve communication in any setting.

Detailing your sensory experiences and broadening your perspective intensifies your fantasies and PMOs. You are more fully accessing your senses that go directly into your emotional system. Remember, the cerebellum, the pain/pleasure systems, and the many sensory relay stations are all part of the same circuitry. When you access your senses, you better access your pleasure systems. Using these techniques is not simply remembering past experiences or creating new fantasies. It is accessing the senses in a way that gives you a full physical and emotional experience that is real in the present. In other words, even though what you are experiencing in the fantasy is not happening in the present time, your body and mind experience it as though it is. If you choose to, this can result in some incredible PMOs.

If your mind perceives something as real, your body will respond as though it is real. A common experience that illustrates this point is one I had recently. I was on a road trip from Florida to Ohio to visit family, and came upon stopped traffic. After a few moments the semi-truck next to me began moving forward. A quick glance up was enough to feel exactly as though my car was moving backwards. Even though I was sitting perfectly still, I suddenly fell over in my seat. I would not have experienced it any differently, either mentally or physically, had I been actually rolling backwards.

Accessing physical memory can bring a stored experience into the present along with the accompanying brain chemistry and other physical changes in your body. Roller coaster addicts experience the intense brain chemistry changes that other thrill seekers crave, the deluge of norepinephrine, dopamine and endorphins that are released throughout the ride. A simulated roller coaster ride creates the same brain chemistry experience even though the "riders" know they are sitting still.

Dr. Robert Heath, Tulane University Medical School in New Orleans, mentioned in Chapter 1, did an experiment with a man suffering from symptoms of paranoid rages. When the patient smoked marijuana, his brain wave activities showed stimulation of the pleasure systems of the brain. Initially drugs do stimulate the pleasure systems of the brain, but, with addiction and abuse, a tolerance is developed and the pleasurable effects are diminished followed by depression and apathy.

Remarkably, the same pleasure brain wave activities that the patient experienced while smoking marijuana occurred when he simply *remembered* past highs (10). Remembering past highs seemed to bring about the same physiological changes that occurred when the patient smoked the marijuana. Basically, he accessed this physical memory, went to the pleasure systems of his brain with thought and his body responded accordingly.

We have natural THC (the ingredient in marijuana that gives the smoker a "high") in our brains called anandamide. Just as endorphins act as natural morphine, anandamide acts as natural THC. Interestingly, chocolate is a chemical cousin to anadamide and binds to the same receptor cell as marijuana. Chocolate boosts serotonin and endorphins and can have a soothing effect on the mind. This can explain chocolate cravings (4) (more on chocolate later).

Another factor that may influence the development of your VRF Super Powers is gender. The routes to accessing PMOs and VRF may be different for men than they are for women. Research verifies the physical differences between the male and female brain. Some of them include: length of the nerve cell connector, pathways that the neurotransmitters follow, density of nerve cell strands, thickness and weight of the corpus callosum (separates the right hemisphere from the left hemisphere), the location of control centers for language, emotions and spatial skills (11).

Women have a thicker corpus callosum. Information may more readily flow between the two hemispheres. This is believed to be why women tend to have the ability to accomplish multiple tasks simultaneously (11).

Men and women process sensory input differently. In general, women have a stronger sense of smell and taste, better hearing and greater touch sensitivity. Men tend to have better distance vision and depth perception while women have better night vision and visual memory.

These differences may have an impact on using the sensory imagery to access PMOs and VRF. Women may be better at visual imagery and accessing physical body memories. Men may utilize their strengths of being good at visual sexual stimulation and sexual fantasy. We all have a wealth of sensory experiences stored that we can draw upon at any time.

Steps to Virtual Reality Fantasy

Step 1. Choose a Fantasy

When you access PMOs, you are recalling past physical memories that accent the sense of touch. VRF goes a step further by focusing on all the sensory experiences in detail, including touch. To begin VRF, decide on a particularly exquisite past sexual experience that you remember clearly and focus on the sensory details. Do not choose a past experience where painful emotions are attached, as in the break up of a relationship. Choose a pleasurable, happy experience.

In this situation, you are not making up a fantasy, but recalling a past real happening. That means all of the sensory experiences related to this time are stored in your memory basin and can be accessed and re-experienced in the present.

Summary – Step 1: Choose a past sexual experience, create a fantasy, or combine a past sexual experience with fantasy and change or enhance it to your liking. You may find a real past experience easier to start with because you will be recalling from memory. When you begin creating fantasies, let your imagination run free.

Step 2. Experience the Fantasy from Your Own Perception (First Position) Starting with Your Dominant Sense

Start with your more dominant sense (sight, sound, touch, smell or taste) and give as many sensory descriptors as you can recall about your past experience.

For instance, if you are a visual learner, close your eyes and "see" the person with you through your eyes (first position). What does he/she look like? Give as many visual descriptors as necessary for you to see this person in great clarity. If the image is in black and white, change it to color. Adjust the tone until the color is crisp and sharp. Bring the image close to you. Give yourself a panoramic, larger-than-life view. Then, make the image the size that feels most comfortable to you.

Summary – Step 2: Experience the fantasy from your own perception (first position) and starting with your dominant sense (sight, sound, touch, smell or taste), recall as many detailed sensory descriptors as you can.

Step 3. Continue Your Fantasy from Your Perception and Recall *all* of the Sensory Descriptors

Stay in first position and focus on the other four sensory descriptors. Don't leave anything out! Describe it as though you are telling your best friend about every tantalizing detail the next day, or writing it as the next best selling romance novel. What are the background noises? Is there music? Rain? What is your partner saying to you? How is he/she saying it? What is the tone of voice? What emotions are being expressed? Can you hear the breathing? Keep going until you run out of auditory descriptors.

What smells are in the air? What is this person's own unique smell that no one else has? Describe every taste you can remember. Exhaust your descriptors.

Think about the touch. What did you feel physically? Recall every detail. What did you feel emotionally? Take your time and feel it again.

Summary – Step 3: Continue from your perception and recall all the sensory descriptors. Go through the other four senses until you feel yourself immersed in the experience.

Step 4. Give Your Experience Verbal and Physical Anchors and Practice Recalling Them

Using the steps you learned in the previous chapter, give

these physical memories a verbal and physical anchor and bring them into the present. Practice letting these feelings subside, and then use your verbal and physical anchor to recall them in the present. Your VRF can have the same or greater intensity as the initial experience, as well as heightened awareness. This reinforces the association between the anchors and physical memories. It also strengthens that neurological pathway helping you develop easier accessibility, or unconscious competence.

Summary – Step 4: Once you are fully re-experiencing these physical memories in the present, give them a verbal and physical anchor (Ch. 3). Let the experience fade and practice recalling it into the present. Access PMOs if you wish.

Step 5. Change Perceptions and Go Through the Steps Again

To increase your awareness and enhance your VRFs, you can go through the same steps, but view your fantasies from the second position. Imagine what your partner is thinking, seeing, hearing and feeling. When you are creating fantasies or elaborating on remembered past experiences, you can expand greatly using the second position.

Next move into the third position. The fantasy can unfold as a love scene in an engaging movie, mesmerizing you. What do you see or experience that you weren't aware of before? When you are ready, move back into first position to feel the full impact of your VRF. As in any life situation, when we view something from only one perspective it limits us. Imagine a director using only one camera angle to film a motion picture. Perceptual positioning adds depth and color to your VRF experiences.

Summary – Step 5: Go through the steps again using the other person's perception (second position), and an observer's perception (third position) as though you were

watching a fascinating love scene in a movie theatre. Then, move back into first position to heighten your awareness and intensify your experience.

Summary of complete steps to Virtual Reality Fantasy:

Steps to Virtual Reality Fantasy (VRF)

1. Choose a past sexual experience, create a fantasy, or combine a past sexual experience with fantasy and change or enhance it to your liking. You may find a real past experience easier to start with because you will be recalling from memory. When you begin creating fantasies, let your imagination run free.

2. Experience the fantasy from your own perception (first position) and, starting with your dominant sense (sight, sound, touch, smell or taste), recall as many detailed sensory descriptors as you can. (See submodalities Ch. 4).

3. Continue from your perception and recall all the sensory descriptors. Go through the other four senses until you feel yourself immersed in the experience.

4. Once you are fully re-experiencing these physical memories in the present, give them a verbal and physical anchor (Ch. 3). Let the experience fade and practice recalling it into the present. Access PMOs if you wish.

5. Go through the steps again using the other person's perception (second position), and an observer's perception (third position) as though you were watching

a fascinating love scene in a movie theatre. Then, move back into first position to heighten your awareness and intensify your experience.

Once you have developed unconscious competence in accessing VRFs, you may begin to move into created fantasies. These VRFs may include all or portions of past real experiences, or past real experiences edited and enhanced, limited only by your imagination

Use your remote control skills and any anchors you have associated with any specific physical or emotional desired states at any time during your VRFs, mixing and matching as you go. The better skilled you become at VRFs and PMOs the more varied and interesting your real and imagined sexual encounters will be.

These techniques can challenge our awareness and level of consciousness. Much of what occurs around us goes unnoticed. Our sensory abilities grow dull out of a need to delete or filter out stimulus input that would otherwise overload us. You can practice using submodalities with any sensory experience throughout your day. Spend a few moments looking at the sky. Really look at it and focus on the colors and shapes. Pay attention to everyday noises. What do you hear that would have previously gone unnoticed? Pick up a leaf and notice its texture, smell and color.

If you are like most, you are probably already overwhelmed and stressed with the daily pressures of living. Most of what we do is what we feel we have to do, rather than what we want to do. However, we choose what we pay attention to and we can develop a greater awareness of the incredible sensory experiences around us. We can choose to "wake up" and live life more fully. Sharpening your sensory abilities in daily life will help you become more sensual during times of sexual intimacy.

Virtual Reality Fantasy with Your Partner

Using VRF in real sexual encounters helps stimulate creativity and can magnify the pleasures. You can have any setting or play any role you create. You write the script, and you are the director.

If you are not comfortable pretending out loud, you can have any dialogue you want in your head. This can increase the excitement for you and your partner without him or her even knowing about your fantasy. Being completely in touch with your sensory experiences and knowing how to reach your MOP gives you a sense of empowerment and sexual confidence. Your partner cannot help responding to this highly intense sexual and emotional energy.

Virtual Reality Fantasy is intended as a fun and very pleasurable skill you can learn to enhance present relationship(s) or entertain only you, as the case may be. It is not meant to take the place of real relationships or people. PMOs are not reliant upon sexual thought or fantasy, but may be heightened by them. There is no right or wrong way to do it, except what you feel is right or wrong for you. It is also up to you whether or not you wish to share your VFRs with your spouse/partner. Use your best judgment.

Chapter Five

RELATIONSHIP SUPER POWERS

*If you do what you've always done,
you'll get what you've always gotten.*

Anonymous

The Brain Chemistry of Love

Are you presently in love? Most of us have experienced the feeling of being in love at least once in our lives. Some of us have been in love multiple times. It can be an emotional euphoria that is difficult to describe and even more difficult to resist.

Of all the words that have been written, sung or spoken to convey the essence of love, little has been said about what that magnificent feeling of love is and what causes this feeling. When two people are attracted to one another, a chemical reaction happens in their brains. At center stage is PEA. This is a substance in the brain that causes elation, exhilaration and euphoria (7).

A synthetic form of PEA is in chocolate, diet soft drinks and over the counter diet pills, though synthetic PEA isn't nearly as potent as the natural PEA your brain produces. Not only does chocolate boost mood, it has antioxidants (4). If you are a chocolate lover, imagine being able to have the pleasurable experience (brain chemistry release) of chocolate any time you please, without ever putting any in your mouth. How many times would you take a "bite" if you didn't have to worry about calories, fat grams or carbs? PMOs give you as much natural PEA as you want.

Could you choose who you fall in love with once you have the power to increase your PEA at will? It's a thought. This Super Power might prove beneficial to those who repeatedly fall for people who are not good for them.

We feel infatuation when neurons in the limbic system become saturated or sensitized by PEA. PEA acts as a natural amphetamine (6). Women usually have higher PEA levels than men. Does this mean women feel love and emotional attachment stronger than men do? It might help explain a few things. PEA also increases at time of ovulation. A women's sex drive usually peaks mid-cycle and around ovulation. The feelings of infatuation result from the neurons in the limbic system becoming bathed in PEA and other pleasure brain chemicals.

Other chemicals released by the brain when feeling in love are norepinephrine and dopamine. These naturally occurring stimulants flood the emotional centers of the brain and can explain why lovers can go without sleep and food for long periods of time and feed off each other. This also accounts for the feelings of extreme happiness and preoccupation with the person you are in love with.

After the infatuation or in love stage begins to wane, your love relationship enters the attachment stage. Love is felt as a more secure, warm and comfortable feeling. A new chemical system takes over (7). The primary natural brain chemical during this time is endorphins. Endorphins reside at the brain's nerve endings and pool in specific areas of the brain, like PEA. But, where PEA acts as a stimulant, endorphins calm the mind, kill pain and reduce anxiety. This chemical activity affects the brain's pleasure systems and is the reason we feel as we do when we are with someone we find attractive.

Vasopressin is a hormone that is produced in the septal region of the brain. The septal region is the center of the pleasure systems we have been talking about. It is where orgasm is generated. Vasopressin relies on testosterone for its sexual effect. It is the chemical associated with monogamy in relationships (6).

In general, the older you get the easier it is to remain attached to someone. If you are in a romantic relationship in the stage of attachment, PMOs can give you the option of having both the exhilaration of in love feelings as well as the comfort and security of a deeper love relationship. You can have both.

Have you ever found yourself involved with someone that you later asked yourself "What the hell was I thinking?" Family and friends may have tried to tell you, but you didn't see it. When you are in a state of intense emotion and your body and mind are flooded with indescribable pleasure, you aren't thinking. You are immersed in feeling both physically and emotionally. It isn't until later, when that intensity begins to subside, that you use the part of your brain that houses logic and reason.

The end of infatuation is also physiologically based. One theory is that the brain cannot maintain this revved up state indefinitely. It is possible that the nerve endings become habituated or the level of PEA begins to drop. It might be like driving your car at 100 miles an hour. Sooner or later you have to slow down even if it's because you ran out of open road and came into traffic, or you need to refuel. PMOs give you more control over this process.

When you are accessing these brain chemicals naturally through PMOs, and through other techniques you are going to learn about, it is typical to use them frequently at first. Lab animals that had electrical stimulation to activate the pleasure systems of the brain pressed the lever that juiced their pleasure systems until the point of exhaustion and choose this activity over food and water.

People are less susceptible. Just like the time(s) you fell in love and thought you might live in your bedroom forever, your body and life adjust and you go back to the things you normally do. Though you may find your norm will be moved up a few (or perhaps several) notches on the excitement and pleasure scale.

The difference is PMOs are endless, unlike some relationships. PMOs can also bring a whole new realm of excitement and possibilities to a relationship.

Love/Relationship Addiction

In our American society, a great number of "in love" relationships don't make it to the attachment stage, or, if they do, it's often not for long. The excitement and intensity of emotional and physical feelings associated with being in love can be such a strong pull, that when it begins to wear off, it is taken as a signal that it isn't true love and the relationship ends.

The initial strong physical and emotional feelings at the beginning of a relationship can feel so good, that many people begin and end relationships based on when those feelings start and stop, thus resulting in unsuccessful, serial relationships. People who tend to do this are often referred to as "love junkies". A softer term is "love addict" or "relationship addict."

Love addiction can be more than emotional neediness or dependency in a relationship. It can truly be a physical addiction to that person who activates the pleasure systems of your brain. A particular brain chemistry "cocktail" develops when you are in love and can be triggered in you when you are with the person you are in love with. A craving for that "in love" feeling, and the PEA, dopamine and other feel-good brain chemicals that are released when you are in love, can develop and a break up of the relationship can result in withdrawal symptoms as in any other addiction.

MAO inhibitors, a form of antidepressant medication, can increase PEA levels and help people who are love sick, or going through withdrawal (8). Having your own ready access to PEA through PMOs can also help. If you can access these natural pleasure chemicals anytime you want, you may be less likely to become addicted in a relationship, and better able to get over someone if it ends.

The process of human attraction is multifaceted. You may have found that the ones that hit the bull's eye of your pleasure systems have some commonalities. We all have personal preferences in terms of physical appearance, personality, backgrounds and interests when we choose a love interest.

Unresolved family issues and patterns from childhood tend to play themselves out in our adult relationships. Whether this is good or bad depends on the issues and patterns. If a parent or caregiver was emotionally and/or physically absent, you may be attracted to someone who has some of those traits like chemical dependency or workaholism. You may attempt to draw and keep this person close to you with the hopes of having that happy-ever-after ending you desired so much as a child.

As a therapist, I often see generational patterns that continue to be repeated like a stuck phonograph record. The song is never completed. It just starts over and continues to stick in the same spot each time, just as a new relationship starts and gets stuck where the unresolved issues lie. Without resolution, the patterns continue.

Being attracted to an emotionally unavailable partner is a common theme in relationships. You may believe that if you love this person enough, it will bring him or her emotionally close to you forever. When you can't get through, you assume you are doing something wrong and you keep trying various ways to reach this person. Only it never seems to work. If you take sole responsibility for the relationship, you have the illusion that you have the ability to fix it. It gives you the fallacy of control.

Usually in this type of relationship there will be glimmers of light, moments of getting your needs met and feeling happy that inspire you to hang in there. You don't stay because of what you have. You stay because of what you hope to have, or maybe you stay because you hope to regain what you felt you once had.

There is generally a fear of being alone and abandoned. Ironically, in a relationship with someone who is emotionally unavailable, you may feel more alone with that person than when you are physically alone. If you are drawn to emotionally unavailable people, you may discover you have a fear of intimacy yourself. It might not seem that way. You may think that your problem lies more in sharing your emotions too much and if only the one you love would feel the same for you, life would be all you ever wanted it to be. It's safe to be intimate with an emotionally unavailable person. It's being intimate with someone who can love you back that's the trick.

Another common theme or pattern in relationships includes a tendency to sabotage when things are going well. This can be out of a fear of abandonment and a belief that being left alone would be unbearable. Feelings of insecurity can escalate and result in behaviors that can negatively affect the relationship. You want closeness, but do things that push people away. You can make excessive or unrealistic demands and ultimately create what you expect to receive — rejection.

Trust may be a primary issue. Maybe your experiences have resulted in the development of a filter that says people can't be trusted. When someone is actually trustworthy, you don't believe it and reject that person before they reject you. This may also come out of a core belief that you are unlovable or defective in some way, a common and very limiting belief.

If you find your relationships all turn out with the same sad ending, look for the common denominators. They are there. What generational family history are you repeating? It is similar to watching a sad movie over and over again, and each time you watch it you unrealistically hope for a different outcome—the happy ending. As long as you choose the same type of person who can't give you what you need, the ending will not change any more than the end of the movie will change. Is it time to change your "filter"? It may be getting pretty clogged up about now.

There are relationships that are toxic to you and those you love. You can become conditioned or habituated to dysfunctional people and their behaviors. There may be a portion of good in them that you love and live for, but the negative side may take over until there is only a sliver of good left in the relationship. You can have an eclipse in your conscious awareness that can last for years. You may learn not to see the pink elephant in your living room. You can walk or tip toe around it, but you will still have to clean up the dung. You may be spending a disproportionate amount of time and energy trying to change the one you love. You can't change anyone else, but loving someone who is bad for you can certainly change you.

What are some clues? Friends and family may show concern for you, and tell you that you are not yourself anymore. You may find yourself depressed and anxious much of the time. Are you so preoccupied with your partner that you are giving up your goals, wants and needs to fill his or hers? Are you keeping secrets about the unsavory details of the relationship from family and friends, and spending less time with them?

People with strong abandonment fears often find themselves in relationships where their partner is dependent on them in some way, such as through chemical dependency or mental health problems. If you are indispensable to your partner it's a sure bet he or she isn't going anywhere. You might ask yourself what needs of your own you are meeting by staying in this relationship. Is it worth the price? There may be healthier ways to get your needs met.

A client shared the imagery she uses to let go of a bad relationship. She said every time she finds herself holding on tightly when she knows it is the wrong thing for her, she imagines she is holding on to a rope and the friction is burning her fingers so she has to turn it loose. Use whatever imagery works for you.

You might say: "But, I am not attracted to the reliable (boring) nice guys." I believe you. Luckily for us there are more than two types of guys/gals out there. In a codependent relationship, you are looking outside yourself to get your needs met. You could be looking for daddy or mommy in all the wrong faces. We tend to gravitate towards the familiar even if it is bad for us. It's as though we see through special glasses that can only see abandonment, rejection or whatever the issue may be. Due to earlier experiences and expectations of that result, we create the very situations we most fear. We tend to delete or discard anything or anyone that doesn't match that pattern.

There can be some deep-seated reasons for this. If this pattern developed due to feelings of rejection or abandonment by a parent who was emotionally unavailable when you were a child, the love you receive in any adult romantic relationship may not "count" unless it comes from someone who is also emotionally unavailable. Of course, this is a paradox because someone who is emotionally unavailable can't give you what you need. If you hang your validation as a lovable and worthy person on this expectation, you can see what will happen. That's why the change has to come from you.

An important part of unsticking this record and resolving old conflicts is forgiveness. The stuck phonograph record can be related to emotional childhood pain that continues to hurt you today. Most parents do the best they can with their abilities at a given point in time. Many adults have unmet dependency needs from their own childhoods, and are so needy themselves that they may not even recognize the needs of their children. Not an excuse because there is no excuse, but a fact. We all change over time.

There is great power in the art of forgiveness, whether it is forgiveness of self, others or both. Certainly, there are acts that you may not find forgivable. If you relate forgiveness with condoning the behavior, then you may not be able to forgive. When you can make the distinction between forgiving and condoning, you can release the pain and unburden your heart and soul. You can let it go and move forward.

You can develop or maintain a relationship with someone who has hurt you in the past based on the present and the future, even if you cannot forgive them for the past. Life is short and unresolved conflicts can literally eat us up from the inside out, making it even shorter. However, forgiveness doesn't mean subjecting yourself to someone who continues the same hurtful behaviors.

Ask yourself these questions. If I made a list of hurts I experienced due to someone else's actions, how long would the list be? What would it include and who would be on my list? Do I still feel the pain today? If so, how is it affecting my life?

Without gaining insight into the underlying issues that keep us stuck, we find ourselves "unlucky" at love and may feel doomed to not only repeat history, put pass it on to our children. Understanding the normal progression of romantic relationships can also help. Just as individuals have life cycles, relationships have love cycles.

The Stages of Love – Making it Last

Stage 1: Attraction/Dating

The first stage in a romantic relationship is the attraction/

dating stage. Your pheromones and hormones are at work. You may see someone across the room and feel zapped as though you were struck by lightening, though falling in love isn't always instantaneous. When you are falling in love, you want to be with this person more and more.

Stage 2: Infatuation/Falling in Love

The second stage is infatuation or falling in love. You have the giddy and delicious effects of brain chemicals such as PEA and dopamine flowing freely. You feel obsessed and cannot stop thinking about him/her. You want to be together constantly.

The person you are in love with first appears perfect in every way — almost. Your brain tends to selectively delete the faults you do pick up on. Your brain filter is taking in what it wants to, hearing what it wants to hear, and seeing what it wants to see. Thus, love is truly blind.

In actuality, you are projecting all your fantasies, hopes and dreams onto this person and believe he or she is the one for you. You are incredibly happy.

Stage 3: Death of a Fantasy

Then life starts to seep in. This is the third stage of romantic love. I refer to this stage as Death of a Fantasy. Some of the things that were being deleted before gradually, or maybe suddenly, make it through to your awareness as some of those feel-good brain chemicals begin to subside. Your vision begins to return. Those little faults become more prevalent. Some of the things that attracted you to this person begin to bother you.

You may begin to question whether or not you are making a mistake. You may feel hurt or betrayed and feel as though the one you love did not present himself/herself honestly. Generally, this is true of both parties. Anyone in a new relationship wants to make a good impression. The range of misrepresentation can vary greatly from likes and dislikes, to already being married.

You may ask yourself why this always seems to happen to you, and when will you ever find the "real" Mr./Ms. Right. This is a critical stage in any romantic relationship. It is the stage that can often make or break the relationship. This is when many people bale out, and seek the next "right" person for them.

Love addicts often start back at Stage 1 with a new partner. If this continues, a pattern of relationship addiction can emerge. If you truly love this person and there are not compelling reasons to get out of the relationship, you may have much to gain by working through this stage.

Stage 4: Attached Love/Productivity/Family

If your relationship doesn't end at Stage 3, you will find yourself here at Stage 4. This is the stage of attached love where couples generally go through their more productive years building a life and family together. Couples become so busy and caught up in the daily demands of living that they often grow apart. The excitement may not be there, at least not in the same way.

The relationship can take a backseat to raising children and building a career. Those faults you detected in Stage 2 of your relationship now make you crazy. There are couples that go through this stage of their relationship still feeling in love and happy, but for most there is a mixture of all of the above. If couples don't have enough intimate and romantic time there is generally less touch. This is going to decrease the oxytocin that helps bond them together. If they are frequently angry at each other, they may not want to touch.

If either or both persons are going through perimenopause, menopause or viropause, which would fit at about this stage, these hormone changes can also have a serious impact on their relationship.

Trials and tribulations are a part of life. Sometimes they bring couples together and sometimes they tear them apart. What are your beliefs about marriage or long-term romantic relationships, and are those beliefs realistic? Frequently, we set ourselves up for failure by expecting the impossible, such as someone meeting all of our needs.

In couples counseling, I frequently see couples with little understanding that the other person has needs different than their own. One or both persons are not getting their needs met in the relationship, but they expect it to be solved by a change in the other person. Accepting limitations and differences and meeting their own needs can be an unfamiliar concept to some. It is sharing the hardships as well as the highlights of your life with someone that can give you a closeness that no one else can replace. That is commitment. You share a history together, for better or worse.

There are many reasons a relationship ends. Sometimes it can be a matter of life or death, as in an abusive relationship. Getting out of a relationship when it is detrimental to you or someone else can be a necessity. However, a majority of long-term relationships end for other reasons, such as affairs, problems with children, finances and sex that could possibly be worked out. Unresolved relationship problems can build and, if they are not addressed, can cause irreparable damage over time. Having a better understanding of these naturally occurring stages and the brain chemistry of love can give you a wider array of solutions and options.

Developing the Super Power of accessing PMOs is a skill that places you in the driver's seat of the pleasure chemicals you produce. You can control them. You can feel giddy and in love when you want to, regardless of what stage your relationship is in.

Stage 5: Until Death Do Us Part

This is the stage of love we all hope to get to someday. You work hard for it. Time seems to pass quickly, and when you pause and look back you realize that you have shared a large portion of your life with this person, in some marriages nearly all of it. Hopefully, as you get older, you can kick back a little bit, not work so hard and retire. If you have children, they may be out on their own. If you have made it to this stage in your long-term relationship, you can benefit from the wisdom you have acquired along the way.

Unfortunately, this can be a time of health problems and possible financial difficulties. Your biggest fear will probably be the death of your partner and being alone. Living without someone you have shared your life with is an excruciating loss.

In time, you may decide to begin with someone new. If so, you already know the stages of romantic love, because you have lived them. Hopefully, the partner you choose will know as much as you do.

Loving You

What messages are you giving to others about what you are willing to accept in a relationship? Assess your limits and boundaries. Do you give others permission or inadvertently encourage them to treat you badly? We can accept the unacceptable so often that others don't even think they are doing anything wrong. You may find people usually treat you the way you treat yourself. If you are as good to yourself as you are to those you love what would you be doing differently?

When we focus more on others' needs then we do our own, it is usually because we love them and believe we are being helpful. We are willing to sacrifice our own needs so those we love can have what they want or need. Sometimes that is appropriate, often it is not. Taking a step back and not intervening in others' life choices can be hard to do when you love them and see they are making some serious mistakes. If this is not a life or death mistake, you could be preventing them from learning important life lessons in your attempts to protect them, and result in harm to yourself and your relationship in the process. Are your good intentions really in the best interests of your loved ones? Take inventory.

When being good to yourself can become a habit (unconscious competence), your likelihood of being attracted to someone who is good for you greatly increases. Look on the inside before you look outside.

Chapter Six

SEXUAL ABUSE AND PHYSICAL INTIMACY

*You will have wonderful surges forward.
Then there must be a time of consolidating
before the next forward surge.
Accept this as part of the process
and never become downhearted.*

Eileen Caddy

The Effects of Sexual Abuse on Intimate Relationships

The number of children sexually abused in the USA alone is staggering. Statistics vary and the exact numbers can never be fully known, at least in part, because many children don't disclose, or when they do, they still go unprotected.

Children don't disclose for various reasons. Some of the common reasons are fear they won't be believed, threats of harm to them or their loved ones, fear they will get into trouble, or fear the family will break up and it will be their fault.

Perpetrators who abuse children are skilled at manipulating them into believing they are equally responsible for their own abuse. Some perpetrators of children are physically abusive as well as sexually abusive, but many "befriend" the child and present themselves as loving and caring to a child who may be emotionally needy.

A child may not recognize a sexual touch as abusive. If the sexual abuse results in pleasant physical feelings for the child and they later come to realize the abuse for what it really is, they may feel intense shame and guilt about any pleasure they felt from the abuse.

A child can become sexualized at a very young age and if the sexual abuse continues over a period of time, he or she becomes conditioned to the abuse. It is important to note that even very young children who are sexualized can sexually act out and sexually abuse other children or pets. This is very common and often goes unrecognized as an indicator that the child has been sexually abused, or that the sexual behavior the child is exhibiting is serious. Early intervention can prevent these children from becoming teen or adult perpetrators. Sexual abuse spreads like a virus. It multiplies rapidly.

Some of the issues associated with childhood sexual abuse include relationship difficulties, problems with trust, inability to recognize or set healthy boundaries, problems with body image, low self-esteem and issues with sexuality and touch.

An adult who was sexually abused as a child may have chronic problems with depression, anxiety disorders, substance abuse and eating disorder. This is not an all-inclusive list.

Many women who were sexually abused as children confuse abuse, love and sex. Their basin or memory of their trauma(s) may be very deep. They have made associations with that trauma that can trigger memories or flashbacks when something reminds them of the abuse.

As we know, memories are stored with what we see, hear, touch, smell and taste as well as with the emotions we feel. If someone was sexually abused in a bathroom and the smell in the room was lilac air freshener and the body odor of the perpetrator included alcohol and cigarette smoke, any one of these odors could trigger (negative anchors) flashbacks of the abuse.

A flashback is more than a memory. It is an intense memory that takes you straight into that memory basin of abuse. Your body responds with physical memories as well as emotional ones. Flashbacks can be extremely frightening.

If you are an adult who was sexually abused as a child, your perpetrator(s) may have touched you in particular ways that can be triggered if your sexual partner touches you in a similar manner. This touch can remind you of the abuse and take you into a memory basin that causes you to have the same body and emotional responses you had then.

This experience can be especially problematic if your partner does not know about the abuse or what triggers it. You could go from feeling sexually excited and intimate to very anxious, cold and distant, depending on your responses to the old trauma(s).

Children frequently disassociate during sexual abuse. This means they develop the ability to separate their mind from their body and don't feel emotionally or physically what is happening to them. They can take an observer position, as though it is happening to someone else. With ongoing, long-term childhood trauma this can become a survival technique that becomes a lifetime pattern and results in feelings of alienation and separateness from others.

Disassociating as a child in an abusive situation may serve a very necessary purpose, but, when you grow up and no longer need this coping strategy, it can be a difficult pattern to break. People who experience life from the observer (third person) position often feel as though they are spectators of their own life rather than living and experiencing it themselves.

If the sexual touch received as a child felt pleasant, an adult with this basin may feel the pleasure in a sexual touch from their partner, but feel the shame and guilt they have associated with it. This could interfere with the relationship and diminish the pleasure. The possible triggers and responses are very individual. No two person's experiences are exactly alike.

There is frequently a generational pattern of sexual abuse in a family. Often, the parent or family member that was sexually abused didn't receive any treatment. They may not have even told anyone about their abuse until their child's abuse was disclosed.

"It's in the past and there is nothing anyone can do," is a commonly held belief. Frequent comments are, "It is over. I just want to forget about it." These same people may have some or all of the symptoms/issues previously mentioned, and may not see a correlation between their current problems and the past childhood sexual abuse.

Unfortunately, many parents who bring their children in for sexual abuse treatment do not follow through with treatment. Dealing with their child's sexual abuse can trigger flashbacks of their own abuse and cause the parent such discomfort that they take their child out of treatment. They may tell themselves it is also better for their child to forget about it.

Perpetrators may more easily target sexually abused children that have gone untreated. Many adults sexually abused as children report multiple perpetrators over the period of childhood and adolescence.

Adults sexually abused as children frequently state that not being believed by their non-abusive parent/caregiver was as traumatic as the abuse. One client in a psychiatric hospital seemed more traumatized by her mother slapping her off the back porch when she disclosed her abuse than by the abuse itself.

Women who were sexually abused as children frequently have difficulties in intimate relationships. Some women with a sexual abuse history have little or no desire for sex and may avoid having sex. Others may be at the other end of the spectrum and be promiscuous, by some standards. Many women with a history of sexual abuse are aware of these issues and struggle somewhere in the middle on this continuum.

They may have been conditioned to believe that their value as a person is measured by their sexual appeal. Some women have sex when they don't want to stemming from an inability to set boundaries or fear of being abused again. If you consent, you have some semblance of control. If you have a pattern of having sex when you don't want to, this can greatly affect your emotional well being over time.

Sexual abuse can happen to adults as well as children. Many women think that if they are married or in a relationship with someone who demands sex, forces himself on her, or coerces her into sexual acts she finds wrong or degrading, that this is not abuse because it is with her partner. You can become accustomed to abuse and not recognize abusive situations whether it is sexual, physical, emotional, or any combination of the three

A woman who grows up in an environment where having a thirty-four year old boyfriend when she is fourteen is acceptable may not consider herself abused. At fourteen, she is too young to fully comprehend the reasons the legal age of consent is eighteen.

Of course, many men also have sexual abuse histories. Statistics indicate one out of four girls and one out of seven boys are sexually abused. This is believed to be a conservative number and boys are sexually abused at about the same rate as girls. Boys are less likely to disclose for the reasons listed above as well as those that may be more gender specific. A boy sexually abused by a male may believe this means he (the child) is homosexual. It doesn't mean the child is homosexual. It doesn't even mean the perpetrator is homosexual. The child did not choose to be abused nor did he choose who his perpetrator would be, though he may be manipulated into believing he is an active participant.

If the perpetrator(s) was a woman, a boy may feel "honored" to have the experience (or think he's supposed to) and not recognize it as sexual abuse. Even if the abuse was experienced as traumatic, he may feel it's not "manly" to complain about any sexual experience with a woman. Contrary to popular belief, there are *many* female perpetrators.

Boys may be less likely to disclose for the same reasons men are less likely to talk about any feelings or problems, or go to the doctor when they are sick. When looking at gender differences, there is the debate of nature versus nurture. Nature indicates the physiological differences, including brain differences in males and females, and nurture represents the gender socialization differences.

Men who were sexually abused as children can have problems with touch and sex just as women can. They may be less likely to seek help or to tell their partners about their abuse or what triggers their trauma responses.

Abuse of any kind is about power and control. A perpetrator may have a gender preference but many abuse children of both genders. Sexual stimulation and/or orgasm reinforce the abusive behavior for the perpetrator.

Sexually abusing others is a form of addiction. This was made clear to me when I was working with an adult offender who had sexually abused his 14 year old stepdaughter. He described a feeling of exhilaration when he abused her. I asked if he had ever felt this feeling doing anything other than sexually abusing someone. He thought for a moment, then described the only time he could remember.

He was flying a small plane. It was a clear day and he was relaxed and enjoying the solitude when suddenly the engine died. The plane began losing altitude and he struggled to restart it. The feeling he compared to sexually abusing his stepdaughter was the adrenaline rush he felt just *before* the engine kicked in again.

What substitute activity can match the brain chemistry "thrill" that a perpetrator associates with sexual abuse? Serotonin is one of these brain chemicals. High levels of serotonin are associated with power and domination (10). Levels of serotonin can rise or fall with factors like social status or winning/losing. Testosterone levels are also affected in the same way. Treatment for perpetrators includes recognizing his or her triggers and cycle of abuse.

Regardless of gender, if you have a history of childhood sexual abuse or trauma and you have not had treatment, I highly encourage you to seek the help of a trained professional. Sexual abuse treatment does not have to be re-traumatizing. There are therapeutic techniques that give you distance from the trauma as you are recovering and healing. Addressing how the sexual abuse is affecting your life in the present can also be very effective in resolving old sexual abuse issues. The focus does not have to be reliving traumas of the past.

The following are techniques to decrease your trauma responses in sexual situations. These techniques are for both men and women with sexual abuse histories.

Steps to Dilute Sexual Abuse Trauma Responses

1. **Identify your trauma responses.** What is your response both physically and emotionally when something reminds you of the past abuse? Be specific. For example, if your response includes panic or anxiety, you may feel your heart rate increase, have a sense of tightness in your chest with difficulty breathing, your mind may be racing, you may feel scared and have a strong need to flee. If you "flee" psychologically, you may disconnect from the experience both emotionally and physically, feeling numb and detached. This disassociation may be the way you survived the abuse while it was occurring, but it can cause relationship problems in the present. Learn your specific trauma responses to sexual touch.

2. **Identify your specific trauma response triggers.** Your trauma response triggers are individual. What triggers your trauma responses will depend on the circumstances of your past sexual abuse, what sensory information you have stored and associated with the trauma(s), and what physical memories you have related to the trauma(s). One young girl in treatment had a trauma response of extreme anxiety and panic when she saw or smelled a particular spray cleaner. This was because her mother cleaned for the man who sexually abused her and she used this brand of spray cleaner in his home where the abuse occurred. The mother was not aware of the sexual abuse at the time. The man was eventually incarcerated for the sexual abuse. The young girl did not tell her mother about her trauma response to the spray cleaner and the mother continued to use it, not knowing how it affected her daughter. I encouraged her to tell her mother and she did. The spray cleaner triggered the trauma response, taking the child into her trauma basin with the accompanying brain chemistry she experienced at the time of the abuse. Learning what triggers your trauma response is very important in being able to dilute or diffuse the devastating emotional effects. Your trauma response can be triggered when your partner touches you in a manner similar to the sexual abuse. You may generalize any and all sexual experiences with the sexual abuse and have one large basin that anything sexual goes into. If this is true for you, anything you perceive as sexual can trigger a trauma response.

3. **Discuss your triggers and trauma responses with your partner.** Your partner may be taking your trauma responses personally and not understand what is hap-

pening to you. Depending on what your specific triggers and circumstances are, you can decide whether you want to gradually desensitize yourself to these triggers or avoid them. All triggers may not be avoidable. If any sexual touch triggers your trauma responses, and you have a romantic partner, complete avoidance will probably be detrimental to the relationship. Your partner may be able to help you work through your touch issues.

4. **Set physical boundaries.** Working on sexual abuse issues takes time. You may not be ready to work on the sexuality issues right now. Communicate with your partner. Participating in sexual acts that triggers your trauma responses to please someone else is not beneficial to either you or your partner. In fact, the feeling of being involved in a sexual act when you don't want to be can be a trigger that reminds you of the past abuse. Experiencing any of the dynamics that were in place during the abuse can trigger a trauma response. Pressure to become "cured" quickly can also be a trigger. You may begin to look at your partner as a "bad" guy, associating him or her with the perpetrator(s).

5. **Build a strong basin of positive touch experiences.** Gradually increase your positive touch experiences with your partner to deepen that basin as you dilute your trauma responses (next exercise). You can begin gradually adding more loving touch that isn't sexually motivated until you become more comfortable. This can take a great deal of patience from you and your partner.

6. **Use self-talk.** Learn to recognize the signs of an impending trauma response *before* it becomes full blown. Use thought stoppers, short phrases (verbal anchors) to

stop the negative physical and emotional responses. Tell yourself in whatever words work best for you that the abuse is not happening to you right now. You are safe. Your partner isn't the perpetrator(s), and you will no longer allow the perpetrator(s) to harm you, much less be in bed with you and your partner. Think of a time you felt very strong and confident and bring that feeling into mind and anchor it. Tell the perpetrator(s) to get lost, in whatever language you choose to use. Make a conscious decision to leave that trauma basin and enter one with positive memories of your partner and pleasant experiences you and your partner have shared together. Do this as many times as it takes each and every time a trauma response starts to occur. You are choosing positive brain chemistry over negative. You have a choice and you are in control.

Untangling the Web of Sexual Abuse from Love and Sex

The following is a technique designed to reduce or eliminate a trauma response by separating positive sexual memories from negative sexual abuse memories, in essence creating two distinct memory basins instead of one that combines the two. When you have a childhood history of sexual abuse, the sexual abuse traumas can become entangled with love and sex. The results can greatly affect the quality of life for the individual experiencing this.

You may want to practice these techniques first with a negative memory that is not a part of the sexual abuse trauma, something innocuous, like a disagreement with a friend. After you feel comfortable with it, move into trying the technique with the least traumatic of your memories. If it is too emotionally difficult to do this exercise on your own, find a reputable therapist to work with you. If at any time while trying any of

Sexual Abuse and Physical Intimacy

these techniques you feel a strong trauma response, then STOP. Respect your own boundaries.

To do this exercise, you will use the submodalities techniques outlined in Chapter 4 (Virtual Reality Fantasy) to diminish the negative sensory memories and impact of the sexual abuse.

1. Choose a negative memory you associate with the sexual abuse. Work with only one memory at a time. Recall the sensory details of what you saw, heard, tasted, smelled, touched, or how you were touched. Don't stay there too long. If you are seeing the scene in color, change it to black and white. Put a frame around it like a TV screen. All smells and tastes are contained in that screen. You cannot smell or taste them anymore than you can smell or taste anything that you watch on television. See the screen gradually shrink from a 32" screen down to the size of the face of a watch. Turn down the volume one click of the remote at a time until there is no sound left. The screen continues to shrink. You have to strain your eyes to see it at all. In your mind's eye, you watch the screen become nothing more than a tiny speck that floats up and away from you. You watch with a feeling of empowerment and peace as the speck completely disappears.

2. Next, choose a positive memory you associate with sexual pleasure. If you don't have one, choose a positive memory you have of a romantic touch. If you want to improve your sexual relationship with your partner, then choose a touch that you have experienced with your partner. Again, work with one memory at a time. Use your virtual reality skills to enhance and sharpen the image. Make the experience larger than life, encompassing you like a movie in an Imax theatre. The colors are

brilliant and crisp. Step into the screen and let it come to life. The smells and tastes are exquisite and the touch is exactly what you need. Anchor those positive sexual/romantic feelings and have them ready to recall if you begin to experience a trauma response with your partner. You can access PMOs in the present to strengthen this positive past experience and deepen your positive sexual experience basin.

Continue to build your positive sexual experience basin. Remember, your mind takes you automatically, and often subconsciously, to the deepest basin. Make your positive sexual/touch experience basin your deepest, while diminishing your trauma basin.

There are many variations of using submodalities to treat abuse and trauma. There are some excellent books that can help you reduce and eliminate trauma responses. *Heart of the Mind* by Connirae Andreas, Ph.D. and Steve Andreas, M.A., addresses treatment of phobias, traumas and abuse using NLP techniques. *Introducing NLP* by Joseph O'Connor and John Seymour also offers NLP techniques for treatment of trauma. John Bradshaw's book *Homecoming* addresses healing the wounded inner child and has trauma distancing techniques. These are just some of many.

Diluting your trauma basins can be empowering and transforming. You have the power within you.

Chapter Seven

TURNING ON YOUR WEIGHT LOSS BRAIN CHEMISTRY

Do the thing and you will have the power.
Ralph Waldo Emerson

Setting Yourself Up for Success – A Therapeutic Approach to Weight Loss

Most of us want to lose weight and have tried various weight loss programs and techniques, and they may have worked for a while, but the weight crept back on. Some have been successful at losing weight and maintaining a healthy weight and the rest want to know how they did it, so they can do it too. The weight loss industry is a multi-billion dollar a year business.

Obesity is in epidemic proportions in children and adults in our society. Nearly every monthly magazine geared for women has an attention-grabbing article about quick and easy weight loss. It's the same messages we've always heard, albeit good advice — diet and exercise.

Fad diets only work temporarily. Maybe that's because they are designed so that we can only use them temporarily. Could you eat nothing but cabbage soup for the rest of your life?

We read a lot about lifestyle changes. Lifestyle changes can be hard to make and even harder to maintain. Many weight loss programs don't work for most people because they tend to have a one-program-fits-all approach, rather than an individualized plan that will give each person the best opportunities for success. You are expected to fit into the program instead of the program being designed to fit you. Some programs individualize diet and exercise programs, but the staff is not trained to consider individual psychological patterns or needs that perpetuate unhealthy eating habits. Knowing what your specific patterns and associations are with food is essential in setting yourself up for success.

We all have well-established eating patterns that began in infancy and have become a part of us. They are engrained in our psyches. Our patterns have become habits and we may have only a semi-conscious awareness of what they are. If we do identify them, we often do not get beyond the point of identification and feelings of frustration before we find ourselves slipping back into old habits.

We have patterns of interactions in relationships, patterns of how we express our feelings (or don't express our feelings, as the case may be), patterns of thinking, and patterns of behavior. Just as our universe, planet earth and all things in it have an order that keeps the world turning and life continuing, we, as individuals, have our own order. What determines that order includes our genetic inheritance that gives us certain predispositions, our learned behavioral and our emotional patterns.

Our patterns are well engraved in our internal circuitry through repetition and they can be very difficult to change. Our neurological circuitry is wired to take the path of least resistance, much like a child will go to the parent who is most likely to say yes. So, if our circuitry becomes wired for a particular direction (habits), we often do what comes easiest to us at the moment. It may be an automatic or impulsive response with our subconscious mind in charge.

Setting yourself up for success means working within your

established patterns to get the results you are looking for, with as little change as possible. This is done by utilizing your patterns and gleaning out the strengths in them rather than "throwing the baby out with the bath water."

Even very dysfunctional patterns serve a purpose for us, and may have some good in them that we can use to our advantage. Radical change can feel very uncomfortable. The natural tendency is to do what is familiar. It's like pulling out your old worn shoes and wearing them, even though you just bought new ones. There is comfort in familiarity even if it is negative or self-destructive behavior.

Food is one of our most basic needs and what we associate with food can be very powerful resulting in some of our more engrained patterns. Willpower is a logic/reason function of the brain. Logic and reason are frequently overruled by emotion. This is a part of our physiological makeup, not a choice we made. This hierarchy of the brain was hard-wired into our brains many thousands of years ago and we can't change that wiring no matter what we do.

Our survival wiring has been in existence longer and its very design is to keep us alive. The part of our brain used for logic and reason did not form and develop until much later. We have instinctive reflexes that happen in an instant with no conscious thought. It makes sense that these brain functions would dominate the much slower processes of conscious reasoning.

Understanding brain anatomy is relevant to understanding the difficulty in overcoming learned behavioral patterns. The human brain is typically described as having three basic parts, the hindbrain, midbrain and forebrain. The hindbrain includes the brainstem. The spinal cord is connected to the brainstem relaying sensory and motor input and output. The brainstem's purpose is to regulate our breathing, heartbeat, sleep and wakefulness.

This area of the brain is referred to as the reptilian brain and is the most primitive part of the brain. It is designed to act instinctively to any perceived threat and is critical to our survival. Under certain circumstances this basic instinct can become sensitized and result in impulsive acts that contribute to harmful behavioral patterns, including unhealthy eating habits.

The midbrain carries information between the hindbrain and the forebrain. The forebrain (cerebrum) contains everything else, including the cortex, the limbic system, the thalamus and hypothalamus, etc. The cortex wraps around the rest of the brain. The cortex is divided into four parts: the frontal, parietal, temporal and occipital lobes.

The frontal lobe is where our sense of consciousness is centered. The cortex is divided into two mirror images, the right and left hemispheres ("right brain"/"left brain"), and is divided by the corpus callosum that relays messages between the two hemispheres. Though the right and left hemispheres have the same four lobes on either side of the cortex, they do not function identically.

Logic and reason is in the left hemisphere and the limbic system that regulates emotion and our primary sensory input is in the right. It is through our limbic system that we determine what is real and true. Our survival instincts and basic needs on the right take precedence over the left side.

The limbic system also has the built in pay-off of endorphins, dopamine and other naturally produced pleasure chemicals that logic and reason does not offer us, and this pay-off is immediate. Can you hear the two voices? Limbic system: "Go ahead have some, it will make you feel good right now." In a sing-song voice, "I'll give you candy." Logic/Reason: "Don't do it! It will make you gain weight and isn't good for your health — down the road." Immediate gratification usually wins out. When you put that tasty bite in your mouth, you try to reason with logic and reason with a little appeasement by telling yourself, "I'll only have one," or "I'll give up something else later."

To increase success in eliminating any substance addiction, whether it is food, cigarettes, alcohol or other drugs, it is important to address the functions of the right brain as well as the left. This includes our emotions, the pleasure systems of the brain, memory, beliefs, associations, patterns and our sensory input both past and present. Willpower is a left brain function. Willpower alone usually doesn't work. What we *know* doesn't count as much as what we *do*.

The thalamus is the air traffic controller for all of our sensory information. Beneath the thalamus is the hypothalamus. The hypothalamus sits on top of the brainstem and is part of the limbic system of the brain, as are the pleasure/pain systems.

The hypothalamus is where our appetite control center is stationed. Damage to one part of the hypothalamus can result in no appetite and not eating. Damage in another part can result in total gorging (10). Most of us don't have damage to our hypothalamus, but there are other functions of the brain that affect our eating patterns and associations with food that can be roadblocks for our willpower.

The gender difference in structure and function of the human brain may also affect weight gain and loss differently in men and women. Some of these structural and functional brain differences may explain, at least in part, why women tend to gain more body fat than men do. Typically, women have a stronger sense of smell than men and are more responsive to aromas. Women also tend to prefer sweets (11).

Sugar floods and desensitizes receptors interfering with the natural process of glucose in the body. This interference results in more fat being stored in the body. It also negatively affects metabolism (15).

Our sense of taste and smell are intertwined with our emotions and pleasure systems. What we taste and smell can make us feel happy. Since the olfactory (smell) bulb is in the center of the limbic system, the olfactory nerve fibers go directly and quickly to *memory* and *emotional* structures of the brain. It's this connection of memory and emotion and how our senses trigger it that is relevant in identifying and understanding food associations and patterns.

Early food experiences and the emotions we felt at the time strongly affect our eating patterns today. The smell and taste of certain foods can trigger past memories and emotions we have associated with the food. The olfactory regions are filled with receptors for *endorphins*. Endorphins not only make us blissful, they decrease emotional as well as physical pain. You can see the picture emerging. Let's explore it further.

Would we be motivated to eat anything if it didn't taste or smell good, triggering the pleasure systems of our brains? Can you imagine life without being able to taste or smell food? There are many people that have lost this ability, both my parents included.

My father had surgery and radiation treatments for mouth cancer (cigar related). He has not been able to taste food or smell anything for the past seven years due to the radiation treatments. He says he never gets hungry, and eating and swallowing are very difficult for him. He actually forgets to eat. He would rather not eat, but he knows he has to eat to stay alive. I don't know anyone who loves living more than my father, so he eats, but very little.

Without his sense of taste or smell he gets no pleasure from food and is not motivated to eat. When he eats, endorphins and other pleasure chemicals are not released, at least not in amounts high enough to reward him for eating. Therefore, he is only motivated to eat by his logic and reason, the much less motivating neurological function.

My mother suffered from early onset Alzheimer's disease until her death last year. One of the devastating effects of Alzheimer's is a gradual decrease in appetite and then inability to eat solid foods and, near the end, the inability to swallow or process even fluids. The progressive brain damage that occurs with Alzheimer's affects every function of the brain, including appetite, taste and smell. My mother would say she wasn't hungry, or, "Food just doesn't taste good to me anymore." She derived no pleasure from eating, and eventually she physically couldn't eat or drink anything.

When our sense of taste and smell are in working order, we are motivated to eat and we are rewarded for it by our flow of pleasure brain chemicals. We are required to eat, or we would die. So where does the problem come in? According to a study earlier this year, findings indicate compulsive overeaters have a deficiency in dopamine receptors that requires them to eat more for the same satisfaction people without this deficiency get from eating (30). Research in this area is new. At this time, it is not known whether the reduction in dopamine receptors existed prior to or is a consequence of compulsive overeating.

Addiction to substances whether it is food, nicotine, alcohol and/or other drugs reduces dopamine receptors, which in turn assists in creating the craving that is the hallmark of addiction. The more someone eats/smokes/drinks/drugs, as the case may be, the more damage is done to their dopamine receptors and the more they will crave their addictive substance. The part of the brain that is related to compulsive behavior is also affected in addiction.

Addiction, regardless to what substance, changes the brain and brain chemistry. Luckily, the brain can recover from most of the effects of substance addiction after a period of abstinence, depending on the substance and level of use. A brain naturally deficient in dopamine can predispose someone to addiction. The neurological wiring that began in infancy with our learned behaviors is also an important factor.

There are many variables that influence our behaviors, such as genetics, our early childhood conditioning and influences in our belief system. We learn throughout our lifetime, but the learning that happens as the brain develops in childhood and adolescence is the most formative. The frontal lobe of the brain is not fully developed until about age twenty (15). We learn by making associations and storing them in our memory.

Our brains are also designed to make patterns from our experiences. We carry the patterns we develop in childhood with us into adulthood.

We will look at how to identify your food associations and the patterns formed from those associations. Once you are clear on your associations and patterns, you will learn specific techniques to work within your patterns, not against them.

How to Change Without Changing (Much)

Consider the associations we make with food and how eating patterns can develop. Food that makes us feel good is often called comfort food. Some people have a pattern of eating when they feel emotionally upset, depressed, angry, lonely, bored, or any feeling that creates a sense of discomfort. People who seek food for comfort have made an association between eating food and decreasing emotions they consider negative.

As infants, when we felt the physical pangs of hunger, we cried to indicate our discomfort. If we were lucky, we were held and cuddled during our feedings and we felt loved, full and comforted. An association was made with the rush of endorphins from the taste and smell of our nourishment, and the nurturance, with the sensation and satisfaction of feeling full. The path becomes worn with repetition.

As we approached toddlerhood, we began our venture into solid foods, and "goody" foods, like cookies, candy and ice cream. Most parents want their children to be happy. They can see the smile on the child's face and the excitement his or her favorite food elicits. A common phrase parents say is, "Okay, but just one more."

Let's not forget about when we behaved badly, even though that's not supposed to be the time you get a treat, it often is. You may have heard something like, "If you will stop that crying I will give you a snack."

In the not too distant past, you were given a lollipop after the doctor gave you a shot, along with mommy's soothing. Somewhere along the way, someone decided stickers were a better idea. There are many of us that received our immunizations when they still gave out the candy. This is a minor example of how a food association can form. Some food associations are healthy and some are not.

Many begin with the best of intentions. Bedtime snacks are common with children but when this becomes a lifetime habit, it can be unhealthy and a difficult habit to break. Numerous life situations can affect food associations.

If you were not fortunate enough to have that nurturing caregiver who responded to your needs when you were an infant or young child, you may have grown up with a sense of deprivation. There are many children who cry and get no response. There are many families that simply don't have the money or resources to give their children healthy diets and adequate food. Unmet emotional and dependency needs can manifest as food or other addictions in adulthood.

There are many neglected and abused children who don't get most of their needs met, including being fed properly. Even children who grow up without going hungry may not have the extras that many kids have. Food can take on a very serious meaning if you experienced any of these things.

Food can be used as a power and control tactic by caregivers. Food can be withheld as punishment, and children can even be forced to eat food that isn't fit for consumption. I once had a young client whose mother feed him dog food as a punishment.

Children in these situations can learn to hoard and hide food, or vastly overeat when they have the chance because they know hunger is coming later. That primitive part of the child's brain becomes activated frequently keeping them in a survival mode. If this part of the brain becomes overused, or sensitized, that hard-wired response of never feeling full can easily continue into adulthood no matter how much money you have or how full your refrigerator is. The slightest sense of deprivation can trigger this survival response and result in overeating. Even the earliest signs of natural hunger can be a trigger. An established sense of deprivation runs deep.

Most childhood food associations are not trauma related. You may have had a parent who taught you to eat every bite of food on your plate and wanted you to feel properly guilty if you didn't, because there are starving children all over the world. Parents sometimes discipline by sending a child to bed without supper. Another parent may slip food or a snack to a child on restriction. Many children eat anything they please after school because their parents aren't home yet. Families with busy schedules may eat fast food several times a week. Childhood patterns become adult habits.

Parenting styles can play a role in eating patterns, as well as other patterns of behavior. Parents usually fit into one of four categories, 1) permissive, 2) autocratic (overly strict), 3) democratic, or 4) absent (physically and/or psychologically).

A permissive parent isn't good with boundaries or setting limits. They give in frequently and tend to indulge their children. They may have developed a permissive style because one or both of their parents were permissive, or because one or both of their parents were overly strict or abusive and they swore to never be like that with their children. You can become so determined to not be like someone else that you lose sight of who you really are.

An autocratic parent is often a stern disciplinarian. There is not much room for bending the rules. It's their way or the highway, end of discussion.

A democratic parent is more balanced and flexible. This parent sets limits and follows through with consequences, but can bend, depending on the situation. Most of us strive to become democratic parents. We all know there are no perfect parents, and, as parents, we do the best we can.

Absent parents may be physically unavailable due to divorce, death or separation. A parent can be emotionally unavailable due to alcohol/drug addiction, workaholism, depression and/or other mental health problems, or due to a restricting physical illness. A parent can be there physically, but may be psychologically absent from their child's life.

How you were parented can also affect your ability to self-discipline. Setting boundaries and limits and following through are learned behaviors. If you grow up with one autocratic parent and one democratic parent (a common pairing), you probably internalized some of both parenting styles. You may find yourself with an internal struggle where your "inner autocratic parent" tells you that you can't have or do something while your "inner permissive parent" says, "Oh, yes you can!" Very often your inner permissive parent wins out. Not unlike a child who happens upon the opportunity to indulge in junk food until it begins to pour from orifices, you may find this doesn't serve you well.

Anything that represents a "no" answer can feel like external control and be met with resistance. Resistance to what feels like outside control may actually be a response to a lack of internal control.

Without setting boundaries and limits in your own life there is no balance, only extremes. Once this is recognized, you can begin to view setting personal limits and boundaries as a way of giving you more control instead of taking it away, resulting in less resistance and more success.

Let's take a closer look at how to identify eating patterns and food associations.

The Smorgasbord Diet

There are many things that can influence our food preferences. Your ethnicity and culture, or living in a particular geographic area can have a significant influence on your food preferences. You may love a particular food dish because someone you love often made it for you as you were growing up. Your family may have had a particular style of cooking that was passed down from one generation to the next.

Foods you associate with your roots may be calorie laden but also rich with memories and emotions. To give up foods related to religious ceremonies, celebrations and family traditions may seem to border on treason.

My personal "roots" are southern. Southern hospitality means offering a banquet to your guests who then feel obliged to eat hearty or risk being insulting. I have grown accustomed to the feeling you get on a holiday when there are so many choices of delicious foods you don't know where to start first. Therefore, I know when I want to lose weight I have to take this pattern, and my other food associations, into consideration. I am conditioned to think of food in terms of delicious excess and associate it with friendship, love and caring. These are the elements that have to remain in place when I develop a personalized eating plan. I call my personalized eating plan The Smorgasbord Diet.

Basically, the smorgasbord diet is mindfully choosing what goes into my mouth, while at the same time providing myself with so much variety that there is no sense of deprivation. When we remain consistent with our established eating patterns, that feeling of deprivation that makes us run for the fattening goodies goes away. The change is eating foods that don't promote weight gain, keeping some favorites and eating them occasionally, and substituting others with less fattening foods.

If I didn't stay within my engrained eating patterns, I would be compelled to go back to old habits. I know I have a bounty of food available to me whenever I want it. Therefore, my reptilian brain will not put me into a subconscious alarm state signaling to me that I am starving and, instantly and without thought, I put anything I can find into my mouth. It can also be cost-effective by gradually stocking up on healthier choices and not eating out frequently.

The smorgasbord diet also eliminates the inner autocratic/permissive parent conflict that can result in being permissive with myself. This inner permissive parent may be the ultimate definition of "lack of willpower". I am "allowed" to eat whenever I want and as much as I want (from my long litany of healthy foods, and a few unhealthy ones), thus eliminating the inner power struggle and control issues. The results are less resistance. Because I know I can eat excessively, I choose not to.

This does not mean eating tasteless, boring foods. If you have a belief that substituting healthier foods means eating foods you don't like, then you are less likely to try substitutes. Broaden your horizons (and your level of conscious awareness) by really looking at your choices in the grocery store and your favorite restaurants. By making a few moderate changes, I am keeping the elements of my patterns and associations that are meaningful to me, and discarding those that are not in my best interest.

We will continue to explore food patterns and associations to help you define what food means to you, and which associations you make with food. Once you have a clearer understanding of these associations and your eating patterns, develop your own individualized healthy eating plan that is consistent with your food associations and patterns, and that helps you accomplish your goals.

Present Day Eating Patterns that Keep You Gaining

You may have some eating patterns that are completely modern day and not necessarily associated with the past. These patterns are probably more related to your lifestyle, the type of work you do, and so on. Identifying your present daily eating patterns is also imperative to successful weight loss and establishing healthy eating habits. Bringing them into your conscious awareness and keeping them there can increase your opportunities for success.

People often eat when they are tired or thirsty and not always necessarily when they are hungry. Working long hours can mean going beyond regular mealtimes before eating. When this happens you may feel as though there is a gauge in your head that has dropped below the "dangerously low" mark and a red flashing light and alarm going off shouting, "Eat! Eat! You are starving to death!" That's your reptilian brain at work.

That level that drops is your blood sugar level. Glucose levels fluctuate throughout the day. If you don't refuel regularly, it continues to drop until you feel starved. To avoid this, keep your "fuel tank" at least half full.

This usually means eating small amounts of food (from your healthy food list) throughout the day and evening, with at least one larger meal somewhere during the day, preferably midday. If you eat a high protein lunch, you tend to eat fewer calories in the evening. The higher protein seems to trigger hormones that decrease appetite. Don't restrict yourself to very small amounts of food, unless you are eating small amounts frequently.

Most people are not skilled at identifying their own basic needs. They may eat when they are tired instead of resting. They may sleep when they are bored, and so on. A common sense approach to healthy eating is eating when you are hungry and stopping when you are full, no matter how much food is left on your plate. It can take a few minutes for your system to register "full". If you eat slowly and savor your food, you give yourself more time to know when you are full.

There is another reason to slow down your eating. A research study done at the University of Minnesota found that a way to take advantage of the appetite suppressants we produce naturally is by smelling our food before we eat it. The brain has a smell counter that counts how many bites you put up to your mouth (17). We have a chew counter too. It's as though x number of smells and bites chewed equals full. If you take smaller bites, chew longer and take the time to smell your food, you can feel full faster.

Another present day eating pattern most all of us have is eating fast food, dining out, and eating more processed foods due to busy lifestyles. We seem to never have enough time. The average American lifestyle is extremely stressful and harried. There is not enough time or energy to cook often, or even shop well. We are bombarded with advertisements encouraging us to eat out and buy junk foods. It's quick, it's easy and it's fattening.

The fast food industry is not satisfied that we are buying their greasy food as fast as they can make it, they want us to Super size it and Biggie size it and we do, because it's only a few cents more, after all. The more calories eaten, the more energy the brain has to expend to burn the added calories. Burning more calories weakens brain cells and accelerates aging of the brain, while eating fewer calories extends life expectancy (4).

I recently put a half a pecan pie and a perfectly good cherry cheesecake down the garbage disposal so I wouldn't eat anymore of it. Did that make you cringe or gasp? Most of us were taught by our parents not to waste food and may have some strong associations in this area. The pie and cheesecake were left over from a holiday and I knew it would all end up in my tummy. Maybe it was wasteful, but better wasteful than waist full.

You can work within a pattern of "not allowed to be wasteful" by cooking less food, ordering half portions in restaurants, getting a "doggie" bag, putting your food on a smaller plate and not getting more until you give yourself a few minutes to register full. Use whatever methods work for you.

If you eat out, be selective. In either case, stop eating when you are full, no matter how much food is on your plate. You can always take the leftovers home and have them on another day. Without a great deal of thought, you can strategically plan where you are going to eat that has the best menu items for you.

We all have triggers that ignite our negative eating patterns. Stress triggers what I call my "deserving" mode. After a rough day, I may think, " I deserve a milkshake after what I've been through." Then I feel justified.

Identify what form of self-talk (thoughts) you use just *before* you break away from healthy eating. Self-talk can be very powerful. Your words, both internal and external, change your brain chemistry. Your brain chemistry changes your feelings and your actions. The reverse is also true.

Notice what you think and feel before during and after you eat. Keeping written or mental notes of these thoughts and feelings can be helpful. You may find a pattern of:

1) having a feeling(s) you identify as negative.

2) feeling a strong need to stabilize or get rid of those feelings.

3) thinking of eating or impulsively doing so.

4) rationalizing indulgence and feeling deserving.

5) giving in to your craving and enjoying it in the moment.

6) feeling guilty and self-critical afterwards, triggering you back to step 1 again.

If you put this pattern on a graph, it would have a down, up, down pattern, like a roller coaster ride. If you end on down and down is a trigger to go up, you can see what happens.

The more conscious awareness you develop of your triggers and the self-talk you use when they happen, the better you can intervene through reducing triggers and having positive self-talk ready to replace the negative.

The following questionnaire will give you a good starting point in examining your food associations and patterns, as well as other problem areas related to food. Your answers will highlight problem areas and help you develop your Individualized Healthy Eating Plan.

Assessing Your Eating Patterns

1. My ideal weight is _____.

2. I presently weigh _____.

3. Someone my age should weigh _____. Explore any limiting beliefs (Ch. 2).

4. If I were my ideal weight, the negative changes in my life would include
   _____
   The positive changes would include
   _____

5. I take in approximately _____ calories per day.

6. Most of my calories are from _____
   _____

7. I sleep _____ hours per night.

8. I work _____ hours per day, and _____ hours per week.

9. I am physically active _____ percent of the time.

10. I eat fast foods _____ number of times per week, most frequently at _____

11. I eat in restaurants _____ times per week, most frequently at _____

12. I eat at home _____ times per week. I mostly eat
    _____

13. I consume _____ ounces of soft drinks per day.

14. I drink _____ ounces of water per day.

15. I am most likely to self indulge with food when _____
    _____.
    I justify this by saying to myself
    _____.

16. The unhealthy food most difficult for me to give up is
    _____.

The reason is _____.

Potential substitutes for this food include:_____
_____

17. I eat when I feel _____
_____

18. I associate_____
_____ with food.

19. Foods I primarily associate with my childhood include _____

Feelings I associate with these foods are _____

Significant people I associate with these foods are _____
_____

20. If I don't finish the portion of food served to me I feel _____

21. Food I associate with my cultural background or "roots" are _____
Feelings I associate with these foods are_____
_____

22. My family's holiday and celebration food traditions include_____
_____

23. I tend to overeat when I feel_____
_____

24. Hunger triggers these emotions: _____
   _____

25. My average size as a child and adolescent was: small – medium – large.

26. My parents and significant others told me I would be: small – medium – large.

27. I ate _____ amounts of food as a child and adolescent.

28. The messages I received about food as a child and adolescent included: _____
   _____

29. The amount of food available to me as a child and adolescent was _____ most of the time. The feelings this evokes in me are
   _____

30. As a child or adolescent, I would eat to feel _____
   _____

31. The rules about food when I was a child and adolescent included
   _____
   _____

32. My mother's parenting style was: permissive — autocratic — democratic — absent.

33. My father's parenting style was: permissive — autocratic — democratic — absent.

34. Other significant caregivers' parenting styles were: permissive — autocratic — democratic — absent.

35. My parenting style is: permissive — autocratic — democratic — absent.

36. I would rate my present ability to self-discipline as _____ on a scale of 1 – 10 with 1 as extremely low and 10 as extremely high.

37. My patterns of eating that I find hardest to change include _____
_____

38. The way I can work within these patterns and eat healthy include _____
_____

    After you complete the questionnaire, develop your Individualized Healthy Eating Plan based on your answers. Make a list of positives and negatives of your present eating habits. Take note of the things that you are presently doing that are healthy. Maybe this is drinking plenty of water, or not eating fast foods very often. Place your present healthy eating patterns on your positive list. Make a list of your present eating habits that are contributing to your weight problem.
    Once you have your lists, choose one or two items on your negative list that would be the easiest for you to adjust. Of course, continue all your present healthy eating habits. Keep your initial changes small, attainable and consistent with your engrained food associations and patterns. Also, make a list of techniques

that have worked for you in the past. Don't waste time doing what has failed before. The *Developing Your Super Powers Workbook* will give you more assistance in developing your Individualized Healthy Eating Plan.

The Deadly Roadblock Called Denial

Our emotional defenses, including denial, play a major role in our lack of conscious awareness. A majority of our society is in denial about important health issues like obesity, smoking and drug/alcohol abuse. Denial is a part of our natural defense system, wired in like everything else with specific functions to preserve our species.

One of the primary functions of denial is to protect us from emotional pain. As with any body/brain function, we can weather some storms that can throw our healthy denial mechanisms out of whack. We persist in doing things to our bodies that we know are going to damage us, and probably result in our early demise, but we do it anyway.

In Deepak Chopra's book *Ageless Body Timeless Mind*, he refers to a case study by Irvin Yalom in Yalom's book *Love's Executioner*. The story is about a young overweight woman who came to Yolam for psychiatric treatment. Through the course of treatment she began to lose weight, though that wasn't the reason she initially entered treatment. At each new juncture of weight loss, the young woman had dreams and flashbacks about past traumas from a time period in the past when she weighed the same amount.

It seemed that her emotions and memories were stored in her fat cells and as she lost pounds the memories reappeared. As the traumas were resolved, she would lose weight again. Sound hokey? There is scientific evidence that supports this.

In her book *Molecules of Emotion*, Candace Pert refers to peptides, the message carriers of information throughout our body and brain, as "molecules of emotion". Her work indicates emotions and memory are carried by peptides and stored in the body. She states, "Trauma and blockage of emotional and physical information can be stored indefinitely at the cellular level."

Eating disorders at both ends of the spectrum can be related to past traumas. In one of my previous sexual abuse treatment groups there was a teenage girl who was anorexic. Despite her skeletal appearance, she still had larger than average breasts. She told the group that she wanted to lose weight so her father would no longer find her attractive. Many compulsive eaters have the same underlying issues, except food is used to cover up. The impact of thick layers of denial may be more damaging to us than we think, and the benefits of letting go of some of it, may be greater than we think.

Denial fosters addiction. Denial shields addicts from the realities of what their addiction is doing to themselves, others and their lives, thus allowing the addict to continue on a self-destructive course. A word of caution, however, when denial is used to protect us from intense psychological pain and trauma, it is important to respect those boundaries. Professional help may be needed if you have a history of severe trauma.

A common denominator in obesity, smoking and drug/alcohol abuse is addiction. The payoff of addiction is the brain chemical change that releases dopamine, endorphins and other natural pleasure chemicals in our brains. We become so addicted that we believe we can't give up our addictions. It can seem insurmountable, or at best, too hard. We are only comfortable in our body-mind when we have emotional homeostasis. If something is out of balance, our brain and body will do everything it can to self-correct. The brain seeks order. Withdrawal certainly throws anyone out of balance. The physical cravings can be emotionally as well as physically painful.

Logic and reason tells us physical withdrawal is temporary, but we often can't make it through that period without reusing our substance. We want to feel better. We want to feel good. I doubt there are many smokers, drinkers, food or drug addicts who want to get lung cancer, heart disease, have a stroke, or any other terrible thing that can happen to them. So why do they continue using their substance of choice? How do they keep a psychological balance?

It's done through denial and rationalization. "It won't happen to me. If it does, they are coming out with new treatments." "My smoke isn't hurting my child. I grew up with it. It didn't hurt me." "My child is becoming overweight like I am, but he has time to grow out of it." "I'm not as big as her." "I like to drink, but I have it under control." "I can quit anytime I want to, I just don't want to." "My grandfather drank all his life and he lived to be 90!" If you are feeling a little uncomfortable with this topic, it may be an indicator of how it feels when denial begins to creep into your awareness. Denial is like a bat. It is only comfortable in the dark.

When we find ourselves in a situation that is unacceptable to us, we attempt to change the situation or remove ourselves from it. If that is not possible, our mind will begin to find some reason(s) why it's really not that bad, and our perception about the situation will change out of a need for inner emotional calm.

Our denial system is activated by emotional discomfort as well as by physical addiction. We can't seem to give up what we are doing, so we have to somehow make it acceptable. Two basic dynamics with any addiction is denial and a lack of control over the substance. If an addictive substance is taken away without putting anything in its place, there is a sense of loss and a feeling of vacancy inside that can catapult us back into addiction.

Accessing PMOs and other desired states of mind that release your own natural pleasure chemicals can give you that gratification, without putting harmful substances into your body. Turning on your brain's pleasure systems naturally can help you get through the physical withdrawal stage of nicotine, alcohol or other substance(s) of addiction.

Accessing PMOs or other desired states is not a cure-all for any addiction. It can be a viable tool in adjunct with other treatment approaches. We will discuss other addictions and additional treatment techniques in the next chapter. For now, I'd like to further explore denial's role in weight gain and unhealthy eating.

Thin Americans – An Endangered Species?

My older daughter and I owned a retail store a couple of years ago. It was quite a unique store called *Moxy*. One of our specialties was vintage clothing. We called it treasure hunting to go to estate sales, thrift stores and yard sales to purchase one of a kind clothing to sell in the store.

One of the problems, however, was so much of the vintage clothing came in very small sizes. It was always a disappointment if we found a beautiful "treasure" and we couldn't fit into it. (We kept a lot of our treasures.) Why was most everyone so small in the 1950's and 1960's? A size 8 then is about a size 3 now. That says our perception of what constitutes small, medium and large has changed over time.

We become habituated to our physical condition, which basically means we become so used to looking at it that we put our attention elsewhere and don't see it any more. There has also been a gradual change in our society's perception of what constitutes small, medium and large. Our denial system and need to rationalize tells us it is "okay" or, "not that bad."

We usually think of someone with a distorted body image as someone who thinks she is fat when in reality she is life-threateningly thin. *A distorted body image can also be life threatening if someone is minimizing or underestimating their obesity.* What may be an even bigger factor in our acceptance of obesity, however, goes back to limiting beliefs. Beliefs have *everything* to do with achieving any goal.

Refuse to be Fat

The concept of youth, middle age or "old" age depends on your perspective, and perspectives can change. Some beliefs can become very fixed. We set self-imposed limits and think in absolutes. If we believe aging means being out of shape and overweight then it will. If you have this mindset about aging, you can change it to a different absolute. You can absolutely believe that you can lose weight and stay fit throughout your life. State it as a fact, not just as a goal. If you continue giving yourself this message your subconscious mind will accept it as a fact and guide you in that direction, even if it takes time for your conscious mind to believe it.

We are limited by our own thinking and we will probably go on thinking the same way unless we see or experience something that contradicts that thinking. Make it a point to look for the exceptions to your limiting beliefs.

I saw a woman in her eighties on a talk show that was in excellent physical condition. She was of body builder status. I don't remember her name, or even the show. What I do remember is she was an attractive African-American woman and she looked *marvelous*. Seeing her brought something I thought was impossible into the realm of possibility. She is proof that it is possible to stay physically fit all of your life.

Once it is conceivable, it is achievable (like PMOs). If you believe being overweight is out of your control, you won't do anything about it. We don't put out the real effort if we don't believe it is possible.

If you say you want to lose weight, but don't do the things that will get you there, then it is time to look at what is stopping you. There may be reasons you are keeping the weight that you have not consciously considered. Brainstorm about any possible reasons you may want to keep those extra pounds and consider them carefully. If you lost weight would you have more to lose than pounds? What would you gain by losing weight and what would you lose?

Until you make a conscious decision to lose weight, you will make only half-hearted attempts. If you truly want to make a change, address the issues that keep you gaining, and continue to look for the exceptions to your limiting beliefs.

It is past time for a reality check for all of us. We have been duped into *accepting* that addictions are somehow okay even though we know they are not. Obesity kills and can kill the ones we love, including our children. The same is true for cigarettes, alcohol and other drugs.

Are our children's perceptions of small, medium and large going to be even more distorted than our generation's, and will this distortion decrease their life expectancy and compromise their quality of life even more than it has ours?

Explore what types of rationalization you are using to continue your unhealthy eating patterns. Developing your Super Powers is done through a greater awareness, including the realities of what addictions are doing to you and to others. Here are some Super Power techniques to help you gain that awareness.

Unique Super Power Techniques for Weight Loss

1. Anchoring Fullness

Do you remember last Thanksgiving Day? Did you eat a lot of food? Think for a moment how that felt. Recall the physical memories of that "fullness". Make sure you have a very clear recollection of exactly what being completely or overly full feels like. If you didn't eat a lot of food on Thanksgiving Day, think of another time when you did and recall it in the same way. Use all the sensory input and submodalities you need to re-experience feeling very full.

Continue to use the sensory descriptors until you get to the feeling of fullness. You are so full you couldn't possibly take another bite. Now, anchor that feeling with a physical and verbal anchor (Ch. 3). Let it subside and practice recalling it again and again until it becomes easy for you, and your path to fullness is well worn and easily accessible. You can also anchor fullness just after eating a meal and recall it when you want to feel full with less food.

A sense of fullness has its category or basin in your stored memory just as everything else does. You can use your anchor for fullness when you are eating to help avoid overeating. Placing your hand on your stomach before giving in to your food temptations can also be a physical anchor that brings your goal of weight loss into your conscious awareness. You can keep your hand inconspicuously resting on your abdomen anytime you eat as an anchor and a reminder not to overeat.

2. Accessing Your Natural Brain Chemistry to Shift Food Preferences

PMOs give you access to the same pleasure systems as eating something that tastes good without putting anything into your mouth. If you haven't mastered PMOs yet, you can still recall the feelings that release your barrage of pleasure chemicals by remembering and thinking about how it feels in your body and mind when they are present in your system from any pleasurable experience. You can recall any desired state that activates your pleasure systems and use your anchors to help recall them.

If someone says, "I'm getting excited just thinking about it!" in anticipation of an event, what does that tell you about their brain chemistry at that moment? What does the movie review that claims a movie is "the feel good movie of the year" tell you about that movie? What can you think about that will give you the same feel good brain chemistry as your favorite forbidden food?

If a particular food is associated with a pleasant memory of someone you love, then this food will probably evoke more pleasure chemicals than another food that you like. This food may serve as a taste anchor that triggers those warm feelings. If this is a healthy food, then eat more of it. If this is an unhealthy food, you may initially use the food to access this desired state of closeness, but once you learn how to recall the sense of closeness with thought, you can access it without eating the food. You can use other tangible anchors to take you there. A photograph or anything that evokes pleasant memories of your loved one can act as tangible anchors.

You can also teach yourself to release your brain's pleasure chemicals with healthy foods instead of unhealthy foods. Start with a healthy food you like somewhat but aren't crazy about. Where would you place this food on a pleasure scale from 1-10 with 10 being the most delicious? Recall a pleasurable experience as you are eating this food and use an anchor that helps you access your brain's pleasure systems naturally. Then, rate the pleasure of eating this food again.

It may take a few practice runs, but you can find the healthy food you've chosen more enjoyable. You can teach yourself to receive more pleasure eating healthy foods. It takes repetition to engrain this association of pleasure with a healthy food you previously didn't enjoy.

At least some of our food preferences are the result of early childhood conditioning. In the movie Sling Blade, the lead character is a mentally impaired man fed only mustard and biscuits by an abusive parent. As an adult, he could choose any food he wanted, but he still had a preference for mustard and biscuits.

Examine which of your food choices are from childhood conditioning. Trying new foods can expand your food options. You may be missing out on some delicious "skinny" foods. The more foods you try, the more choices you can add to your healthy food list.

3. Staying in Your "Right" Mind to Lose Weight

A technique that can help you overcome unhealthy eating habits has been around for a long time. It is a form of aversion therapy. You can condition yourself to make negative associations with unhealthy foods and drinks just as you can teach yourself to feel good when you eat healthier foods. The negative associations you make can diminish or take away the pleasure you receive when you eat or drink them.

I used this technique to stop drinking cola, resulting in a reduction of about 500 calories per day, enough to lose a pound a week without any other food or drink changes or exercise. Telling myself all the logical reasons I needed to stop drinking cola never helped. A different approach was in order. The "right brain" approach to weight loss acknowledges the power of emotional feelings, engrained eating patterns and associations, sensory experiences and the brain chemistry payoffs of natural pleasure chemicals you produce.

The aversion technique works by associating a negative smell and taste with the food or drink you want to eliminate from your diet. I chose a meat seasoning that has a taste and smell I find offensive. I made a commitment to myself that I could drink all the cola I wanted, but first I had to taste and smell the meat seasoning. I placed a small drop of the foul tasting meat seasoning on my tongue, took a whiff, and took a drink of cola.

Each time I describe it, I relive those negative sensory experiences. Even though I found the combination of tastes and smells disgusting, my caffeine addiction prompted me to try this three times on the first day and twice on the second day. By the third day, once was all I could stand.

My desire for cola vanished and never returned, quite an accomplishment for a lifetime cola addict like myself, and it took only 3 days! Neurologically, my association with cola changed from a positive experience to a negative one. This made a more lasting change than willpower alone ever could. Without it, I would have quickly and easily gone back to the old habit. Should the newly made negative association with cola fade, it would be very simple to strengthen it again.

There are other physical memories that are associated with a cola habit, including the physical action of drinking from a glass or straw frequently. If you continue the behavior of drinking from a glass or straw throughout the day and substitute water or a lower calorie drink for soft drinks, you are discarding the part of your habit that is fattening (soft drinks) and continuing behaviors that have become routine (drinking from a straw/glass frequently). The fewer behavioral changes you have to make, the easier it will be to break bad habits.

When you make diet and exercise changes weight loss isn't always quick to follow. It can take time and persistence. If you count solely on willpower, you may not make it to the point of significant weight loss before returning to bad habits. Right brain approaches not only make external changes in your behavior, but internal changes in your brain patterns and chemistry that can get you past those initial few weeks when you are more likely to revert back to your engrained patterns.

There are many reasons why eliminating or reducing soft drinks is beneficial to you and your children. According to an article titled *Liquid Candy* by Michael F. Jacobson, Ph.D., soft drinks make up 27% of Americans' beverage intake. What is considered a single serving has risen from 6-1/2 ounces in the 1950's to 64 ounces and above today. A twelve ounce soft drink has about 150 calories.

The rise in obesity correlates with the rise in soft drink consumption. Children are drinking less milk and juice resulting in a reduction in calcium and other much needed vitamins. Dr. Jacobson states that girls build 92% of their bone mass by age 18 and cannot catch up later. Only 13.5% of girls and 36.3% of boys ages 12-19 get the recommended daily amount of calcium (29). Caffeine increases the loss of calcium in the urine and can contribute to more broken bones in children and osteoporosis later in life (28). There has also been a rise in cases of rickets, a disease that became almost extinct after vitamin D was added to milk in the 1950's (29).

There are many other health problems related to high sugar and caffeine intake. The heavy marketing and immediate availability in most public settings has effected how we define normal soft drink consumption. We consider consuming large quantities of soft drinks daily as relatively harmless and socially acceptable. The negative effects of soft drink consumption on our health, and the health of our children, will come to light over time. Be ahead of the game.

4. Techniques for Comfort Eating

If one of your eating patterns is to eat in an effort to decrease emotional pain, accessing PMOs and other desired states can help. Start by defining comfort. Each of us has our own subjective definitions and personal experiences that we associate with any state of mind, including comfort.

The steps to access the desired state of comfort are basically the same as accessing any desired state. What emotional and physical feelings do you associate with comfort? Does comfort equal happiness, love or nurturance? What physical feelings do you have when you are in the desired state of comfort? Is your body more relaxed? Do you have a smile on your face? Be very specific.

Practice the physical positioning you use when you feel comforted. You are accessing your memory basin of comfort. Think of one of your most memorable moments of comfort in such sensory detail that you feel as if you are there right now.

Pay very close attention to exactly how this feels both physically and emotionally, and then anchor it with a physical and verbal anchor. Let it subside and recall it again. Repeat this process until your path becomes worn and you can easily access the feelings of comfort whenever you like.

When you feel a sense of comfort, your brain releases endorphins, dopamine and the other pleasure chemicals you've been reading about. Developing your Super Powers includes having a conscious awareness of how any desired state feels to you physically and emotionally and changing your brain chemistry by your thoughts to recall them.

Self observe and identify as many ways to feel comforted as you can. Make a written or mental list of situations or activities when you feel most comforted. Be prepared to pull from the list rather than turn to food when you need comfort.

5. Utilizing Your Subconscious for Weight Loss

Just before falling asleep is one of the best times to give your subconscious mind suggestions of changes you want to make in your life. The following is an imagery exercise for weight loss:

As you lay down to go to sleep, close your eyes and begin to feel your body relax. Quiet your thoughts and listen to your body. Be aware of your breathing and hear the air moving in and out, in and out, until you feel your muscles begin to relax.

Place your hand gently on your stomach and imagine what the fat cells in your body look like. Know that heat liquefies fat. Use your mind's eye to target all the fat cells in your body. Feel these fat cells gradually grow warmer and warmer and begin to liquefy. They are beginning to dissolve and melt away. These liquefied fat cells will gradually be excreted like any other body waste.

You are more consciously aware of what you put into your body and choose not to plump up those fat cells. Each morning as you wake up, you feel lighter and lighter. Your energy is recharged and you feel rejuvenated. You have made the decision to lose weight and you know what to do. You know your subconscious mind is working for you throughout the day and night and as choices are presented, you can trust yourself to make the right ones.

6. Choosing Your Brain Chemistry for Weight Loss and Physical Fitness

The pleasure brain chemicals produced when you access PMOs or experience sexual stimulation can be instrumental in weight loss and physical fitness. You were introduced to some of these brain chemicals in Chapters 1 and 5. You are learning to develop the Super Power ability to release these brain chemicals at will. The following are some of these natural brain chemicals and what they do.

a) **Estrogen and Testosterone** – Estrogen decreases appetite and increases sexual desire. Testosterone stimulates sexual thoughts and fantasies, increases sexual desire, builds more lean muscle and increases with exercise. The role testosterone plays in increasing the sex drive of both men and women can't be emphasized enough. An increased sex drive promotes easier access to PMOs.

b) **Growth Hormone** – Growth Hormone increases lean body mass, reduces fat, increases your basal metabolic rate and increases exercise tolerance. Growth hormone also facilitates youth, increases sexual desire and increases energy. Growth Hormone is increased by dopamine, estrogen and testosterone.

c) **DHEA** – DHEA reduces cholesterol and body fat. DHEA raises your metabolism so you can lose weight without cutting back on food. DHEA levels are higher in thin people. DHEA stimulates the septum (pleasure system) of the brain, works as an antidepressant, and increases sex drive and energy. DHEA increases with sex and exercise. It decreases with stress, alcohol use and as we age. DHEA LEVELS RISE SHARPLY DURING ORGASM. Did I say that loud enough? PMOs give you an increase in DHEA, and if it takes you a little time to get the hang of PMOs, exploring your Maximum Orgasmic Potential and having more sex with your partner can also increase DHEA.

d) **Endorphins** – Endorphins are the body's natural painkillers, and make us feel euphoric when they are released. There are many things that can trigger endorphins. In animal studies, blood endorphin levels increased by 200 percent during sex (15). Accessing PMOs gives you a very direct and quick route to your well of endorphins, as does accessing any pleasurable desired state of mind. Exercise also triggers endorphins.

e) **Dopamine** – An increase in dopamine reduces appetite. Medications that decrease dopamine increase appetite. Dopamine is the pleasure chemical that is affected by addiction to food, sex, nicotine, alcohol or other drugs. It is the "reward" of addiction that overrules logic and willpower. Addiction reduces dopamine receptors, creating a craving due to a need to consume more of the addictive substance for an equal release of dopamine. You have to increasingly use more for the same effect. Exercise increases dopamine. Research with animals has shown that exercise not only increases dopamine, it increases dopamine receptors giving the brain access to more dopamine (30). A brain having fewer dopamine receptors than normal is like being in a cold house and having ten electric heaters, but only one electrical outlet. Developing your Super Powers to naturally release dopamine without substances also has the benefit of accessing your own internal "diet pill" without taking anything.

f) **Oxytocin** – Oxytocin is a peptide that promotes touching and bonding. Just before orgasm, oxytocin levels raise three to five times the normal level. It is increased with estrogen, by positive touch and sex. Oxytocin decreases with alcohol use. Since oxytocin is increased through positive touch and sex, and dramatically increases at orgasm, it is clear how PMOs, and increasing your Maximum Orgasmic Potential, can increase oxytocin. In turn, oxytocin increases dopamine, estrogen, testosterone, serotonin and vasopressin. We know their benefits.

g) **PEA** – PEA is one of the most feel good of the feel good natural chemicals. We already know how PEA can affect us in our relationships. PEA is what gives us that "in love" feeling. PEA hits its peak during orgasm. It is a natural amphetamine and has the effect of a diet pill. It decreases your appetite and gives you energy. It also makes you feel *very* good. Did you know you had it in you? PEA also works as an antidepressant. It's easy to see how PEA can aid us in weight loss and fitness. PMOs allow you to release natural PEA at your choosing.

These hormones and brain chemicals are interrelated. Accessing PMOs can help you in more areas of your life than you imagined, including weight loss and fitness.

Sex is excellent aerobic exercise in and of itself. Orgasm is a full body event. Your muscles throughout your body tighten. If you are female, multiple orgasms result in effortless tightening of your abdominal muscles, vaginal muscles, and buttocks. Accessing PMOs is like drilling for oil and finding gusher after gusher. Why pay money for ineffective weight loss substances that can negatively affect your health when you can access your own natural resources that your body produces, and it's free?

7. Activating Your Motivation

Once you develop a routine of regular physical activity and eating healthier, it can seem easy. You may think, "No big deal. Why didn't I just always do this?" It is developing the motivation and getting started that seems to block people.

There are a number of techniques that may help you tap into the motivation you need. You already have the motivation, but you may not be paying attention to it right now. Paying attention to it means bringing into your conscious awareness what has always been there in your subconscious mind.

It's like looking for something in a dark room with a flashlight because the power is out. Suddenly the light shines on just what you are looking for. Everything you need is already in the room, but the flashlight can't lighten the whole room at once, just as the brain can't think of everything we've ever learned all at one time. We select what we focus on.

Think of times in your life when you have been motivated to do something. There are varying degrees of motivation. Think of a time you were *very* motivated to do something. Think of a time you were *very* motivated to do something and you *did it*.

You have a motivation basin where all your memories of motivation are stored. It is one of your categories filed away in your head. Use the NLP techniques that help you access the desired state of PMOs to help you access the desired state of motivation. Find and pull out your motivation file. Maybe that's a behind-in-technology analogy. Type in your category, push the button and go there.

Use your senses and submodalities (Ch 4) to help you recall exactly how being motivated feels to you both physically and emotionally. What physical memories do you have of this time? Did you have more energy? Did you feel excited?

What specifically do you feel in your body when you have more energy and feel excited? Recall these physical memories. Recall all the sensory detail that goes with them. Now, anchor that feeling of high motivation. Give it a physical anchor (body movement) and a verbal anchor (name). You may have a tangible anchor you associate with a time of high motivation, like something you wore, or a certificate of achievement you earned. If so, use your tangible anchors to access your basin of motivation.

Making the association between your anchors and the desired state of high motivation will help you recall this desired state of mind when you want it or need it. Using the physical positioning or movements you remember from the past when you felt highly motivated, such as your facial expressions or how you stood, may help doubly reinforce the physical anchor.

Smiling is one such facial expression. When dopamine and endorphins are released in your brain, for whatever reason, it causes you to smile. Conversely, when you smile, dopamine and endorphins are released in your brain (7). Particular body movements are associated with and act as triggers for particular chemical releases and states of mind.

Your smile can be a physical anchor to put you in the desired state of happiness. The association between dopamine, endorphins and your smile has always been there. It was built in. You can change your brain chemistry to motivation anytime. Just shine your flashlight on it.

8. Your Scale – A Reality Check

Getting on the scale *daily* is an excellent tangible anchor that can penetrate denial. It also serves the purpose of keeping any added pounds in your conscious awareness so you can make adjustments before they snowball. When you stand on the scale and you see you have lost weight, the rewards can include a release of endorphins and dopamine when your brain chemistry changes to happy and proud. You can get a release of the same feel good chemicals that you get when you eat something that tastes good, but for a possibly more beneficial reason. If the numbers on the scale aren't going down at the moment, or they are going up, continue following your plan and use positive self talk to reinforce your determination. Consistency equals results, and it takes time.

9. Thinking Thin

Use the skills you learned to access Virtual Reality Fantasy to help you envision yourself at your most attractive. Remember the research example of the man smoking marijuana and the changes in his brain being the same whether he was smoking marijuana or simply remembering smoking it? That is the principle here. Visualizing yourself at your most attractive brings that future (or past) brain chemistry into the present and your subconscious mind will begin to quietly direct you to that goal.

You can change your brain chemistry to what it was when you were in your best physical condition. You can do this by accessing physical and emotional memory from a time in the past when you were in that physical condition. If you have never been there, or have unpleasant memories (associations) of that time in your life, then focus on the new improved you of the near future.

Old photographs and clothes you might have saved when you were in better physical condition can be tangible anchors. If you didn't save any, you could go buy something smaller with the goal of fitting into it nicely by a certain time.

Don't set yourself up to fail. Give yourself every opportunity for success by starting with small, very attainable goals. Don't buy a size 5 if you are a size 20. Start with a size 18, and when that fits, buy a size 16 and work your way down to your ideal weight. This serves three purposes:

One, the outfit you choose is a tangible anchor reminding you of your goal to get into shape. It is bringing your goal into your conscious awareness as often as you look at it.

Two, the outfit can help you visualize how you will look in it and how you will feel physically and emotionally when you wear it. It helps you be more determined and resolved not to let your goal of getting in shape go back into the dark recesses of your subconscious mind (slight exaggeration for emphasis).

Three, it is much easier to lose a few pounds than it is to lose several pounds. Nothing motivates more than results. Seeing results increases your dopamine and endorphins and reinforces the behaviors you have used to lose weight, like healthy eating and physical activity.

The better you look and feel, the better you will want to look and feel. You will become more focused on the outcome rather than the effort. The effort will grow increasingly more incidental. Thus, you are setting yourself up for success instead of failure.

10. Physical Activity– The Fountain of Youth – What to Do If You Hate "Exercise"

There is no better present day fountain of youth than being physically active. It not only turns back the clock by decreasing your physiological age, improving your health and giving you more strength and energy, but little changes your appearance more than being physically fit. Dramatic before and after photos of weight loss success stories depict this transformation.

Throw the terms *diet* and *exercise* out of your vocabulary. The associations generally made with diet and exercise is deprivation and hard work, respectively. *Weight loss is a side effect of healthy eating and physical activity.* Shifting your focus to health and fitness rather than weight loss will raise your level of conscious awareness to the incalculable number of choices in good foods and enjoyable physical activity that triggers the pleasure systems of your brain. To do this, try new foods/recipes and forms of physical activity weekly until you find what you enjoy most.

Physical activity releases endorphins, stimulates the growth of dendrites, and increases blood flow to the brain (5). Both the left and right hemispheres of the brain are stimulated during physical activity, helping you better achieve the goal of weight loss.

If you have physical problems that limit your ability to be physically active, discuss safe guidelines with your doctor. Sometimes we allow limiting beliefs about our physical capabilities to deter us from doing things we may be able to do.

Successful goal attainment includes "keeping your eye on the prize." Focus on where you are going rather than what it takes to get there. Clearly see yourself already there and you will automatically take the steps in that direction.

If you hate "standard" exercise but decide to do it, use the technique that helps you associate pleasure with healthy foods

(#2 above) to associate pleasure with exercise. Choose the brain chemistry of pleasure when you are exercising. Trigger the pleasure systems of your brain by accessing PMOs or other physical memories of pleasurable experiences while you exercise. You can teach yourself to enjoy exercise.

Basically, losing weight is a mathematical equation. If you take in more calories than you burn, the extra calories are stored as fat. Learn how many calories someone of your sex, height and age burns on an average and consider your level of physical activity. Is your level of physical activity below average, average or above average? Most people tend to underestimate how many calories they take in. Adjust your equation accordingly. Become more practiced at reading labels and read the nutritional brochures at the fast food restaurants.

You don't necessarily have to carry around a calculator or know exactly how many calories you are consuming, but guesstimate higher than you think it is. If you are guessing you are taking in 2,000, estimate that you are taking in 2,500 and build that into your equation. Keep a food journal for a few days and keep track of your calories to get a better idea. If you average 2,000 calories per day without gaining any additional weight and you want to lose weight, you need to reduce your calorie intake by 500 calories a day to lose one pound per week. You can do this by either taking in the fewer calories, burning more calories or a combination of both.

Interestingly, decreasing calories decreases appetite. If your norm is to consume 2,500 calories per day and you begin to gradually reduce your calorie intake by replacing some of your more fattening favorites with lower calorie substitutes, and your average calorie intake drops to 1,800, you will begin to feel full and satisfied with the reduced calorie intake as your brain and body adjust to the change. If you have trained yourself to need more calories than you burn off, you are going to initially crave more food until this adjustment takes place. The body and mind seek balance and once the adjustment to fewer calories is made, you require less food to feel full and satisfied. Having frequent small meals can help with the initial cravings.

If you decide to do a combination of reduced calories and physical activity, start by doing at last 10-15 minutes of *additional* physical activity per day *no matter what*. It can be anything that gets your body moving (i.e. leg lifts while you watch television, parking farther from the store, a few minutes of additional housework, etc.). Gradually increase your physical activity in ways you find enjoyable. Remember to use your abilities to access the pleasure systems of your brain to help reinforce and motive your physical activity.

Nurturing Your Brain

To fully develop your maximum Super Power abilities, give your brain every opportunity to function at optimal level. The production of key neurotransmitters that affect learning and our emotional states are dependent upon the proper combination of vitamins, minerals and other nutrients in our systems. We will not have an adequate supply of serotonin, dopamine, norepenephrine, acetylcholine and endorphins without the "ingredients" to produce them. Fortunately, in our society, we have healthy foods and food supplements readily available to us.

A reduction in serotonin is related to depression, impulsivity, alcoholism, suicide, aggression and violence. A deficiency in folic acid can result in depression, poor concentration, irritability, forgetfulness, sleeplessness and fatigue. Folic acid can be as effective as an antidepressant medication in reducing depression and can increase the effectiveness of antidepressant medications (check with your doctor before taking folic acid if you are taking anticonvulsant medications)(4).

Vitamins B6 and B12 can also improve mental functioning. Vitamin B6 is necessary to synthesize neurotransmitters like dopamine. We lose Vitamin B12 as we age (4).

Children can be greatly affected by a thiamine deficiency. Symptoms of a thiamine deficiency in children include behavioral problems, hyperactivity, depression, anxiety, and sleep disturbance. A thiamine deficiency can result from a diet high in junk food and soft drinks (4).

Research studies have shown that eating breakfast each morning with a glass of orange juice and taking a daily multivitamin can increase a child's I.Q., possibly due to an increased ability to concentrate (4). Fish oil (Omega-3) has been shown to improve ADHD, speed up learning and increase serotonin (4).

The brainpower necessary for clear thinking, retaining information, staying well, healing, and maintaining a sense of well being, depends largely on what we put into our bodies. Jean Carper, author of *Your Miracle Brain*, powerfully describes what is necessary for a healthy brain and why our present day eating habits cause us undue harm and don't allow us to operate at full power.

Since the structure of the human brain has not changed over the past 10,000 years, it makes sense that "fuel" necessary to keep us functioning well now is the same as the types of "fuel" our very distant ancestors consumed. Fast foods and processed foods were not on the menu then. Nuts, fruits, vegetables, legumes, fish and lean meats are the primary ingredients for a healthy brain and body (4).

Antioxidants strengthen the immune system to help us fight off disease and illness. Vitamin C helps create neurotransmitters (i.e. dopamine) and is a powerful antioxidant. Fruits and vegetables are the best natural source of antioxidants. Some of the highest foods in antioxidant value are prunes, raisins, strawberries, blackberries, blueberries, spinach and garlic.

You may be familiar with some of the natural herbs that can decrease depression, anxiety and help with weight loss. Kava Kava is hailed as "nature's valium" for producing a sense of calm and aiding in sleep. CLA (Conjugated Linoleic Acid) has shown in research studies to reduce body fat and maintain lean muscle mass. St. John's Wort has been effective in reducing mild to moderate depression in some people. SAM-e is naturally produced in the body and has shown in research studies to work quickly, decreasing depression with little or no side effects. SAM-e also has anti-inflammatory properties (4).

Someone suffering from a chronic low level of depression may not be fully aware he or she is depressed until there is a brain chemistry change that lifts that depression. Chronic, low level depression can result in a predominant mood of irritability. If you are not comfortable taking prescribed antidepressant medications, consider one of the food supplement alternatives.

Your choices for vitamins, food supplements and healthy foods are plentiful and varied. Do a little research on what builds a healthy brain and body and use what you can live with. Nurture your brain, your body, yourself.

Chapter Eight

DEVELOPING YOUR SUPER POWERS TO ELIMINATE ADDICTIONS

*Men stumble over the truth
from time to time,
but most pick themselves up
and hurry off
as if nothing happened.*

Sir Winston Churchill

Know What You Are Consenting To – Facts on Cigarette Smoking

A vast number of people in our society are addicted to one or more substances. At a workshop on child abuse I attended many years ago, the trainer stated child abuse could be eradicated if alcohol and drug addiction could be eliminated. While that may not be completely true, the devastation to lives as a result of addiction, including cigarettes, is astronomical.

Three million people die worldwide each year due to smoking, and approximately 419,000 of those preventable annual deaths occur in the USA (57). Smoking cigarettes kills more people each year than AIDS, alcohol, drug abuse, car accidents, murders, suicides and fires combined according to the Center for Disease Control.

The decreased life expectancy for the average smoker is a loss of approximately 20 to 25 years (56). Are the big tobacco companies lulling us into submission much like the Pied Piper? Can you imagine the outcry and uprising there would be if terrorists spread poisons through chemical or biological warfare and killed that many people per year, or even in one year? Would we allow our food supply to contain the level of carcinogens that cigarettes contain?

Tobacco is not federally regulated so the tobacco companies do not have to tell us the ingredients in cigarettes. The Federal Trade Commission tested cigarette smoke and found approximately 5,000 chemicals with at least 40 known human carcinogens in it. Some of these chemicals include:

Acetone – a solvent in nail polish remover

Cadmium – a highly poisonous metal used to make batteries

Carbon Monoxide – a poisonous gas

Formaldehyde – a preservative for dead bodies

Hydrogen Cyanide – a respiratory enzyme poison used in gas chambers

Ammonia - Added to enhance the effect of the nicotine causing it to go rapidly into the lung tissue and throughout the body quickly, similar to freebasing cocaine (47)

Cocoa - Another additive to cigarettes that may sound harmless, but when it is burned it produces bromide gas that dilates the airways and increases the absorption of nicotine (47)

Arsenic – A highly toxic poison

Polonium-210 – a **radioactive** substance that originates from the radioactive elements in the fertilizer and in the soil used to grow tobacco. Polonium-210 emits ionizing alpha radiation, the same type of radiation given off by atom bombs. Radioactive isotopes are inhaled deep into the lungs. A smoker that smokes 1-1/2 packs of cigarettes per day for a year would be exposed to the amount of radiation in about 300 chest x-rays. Polonium-210 and Lead-210 (also in cigarettes) has a half-life of over 20 years. It takes these substances over 20 years to change into non-radioactive substances. In the meantime, if you continue to smoke, this radioactive material accumulates in your lungs and travels through your bloodstream. It is also emitted into the air through second-hand smoke and inhaled by anyone who comes into contact with the smoke (51, 61).

Cigars and pipe smoking pose the same risks as cigarettes and the same toxic chemicals are ingested into the body with smokeless tobacco.

The tobacco companies began using additives in the 1950's to increase the effects of nicotine. Tobacco was genetically engineered to make the nicotine in cigarettes more potent (52). They recognized that if there was not an addictive factor to cigarettes, people could easily quit. The tobacco companies also need 4,000 new smokers per day to take the place of the smokers who die as a result of smoking (58). Among other groups, cigarette companies target the young. It is economically more viable, at least for them. One way they are targeting the young is with the new candy flavored cigarettes that children and teens may find more enticing.

The tobacco industry's response to the public concern regarding the health hazards of smoking, when that correlation was made in the 1960's, was to develop and market low tar or "light cigarettes". This kept many people smoking who otherwise would have quit by giving the smoker the *illusion* of a safer cigarette.

The machines that measure the tar in cigarettes do not give accurate readings because the machine cannot simulate exactly how people smoke. Smokers may compensate for the lower tar and nicotine by inhaling more deeply or increasing the number of cigarettes they smoke per day. A smoker may also cover the vents in the filters with their mouth or fingers and the machine measures with the vents unobstructed (67).

Nicotine is the drug in tobacco that causes addiction. Nicotine is literally a poison and is used as a very effective insecticide. Nicotine is as highly addictive as heroin and cocaine. It reacts in the brain the same way those drugs do. Studies show that animals cannot tell the difference between the effects of nicotine and the effects of cocaine (50).

The Brain Chemistry of Cigarette Smoking

It takes nicotine about seven seconds to reach the brain (51, 53). One of the unique qualities of nicotine is that it works as both a stimulant and a sedative on the central nervous system. Nicotine is similar in shape to the neurotransmitter acetylcholine, a brain message carrier, so it attaches to the acetylcholine receptors and stimulates the central nervous system.

This causes an immediate release of epinephrine and an increase in serotonin. There is also a sudden release of glucose, and nicotine triggers the release of dopamine causing it to linger longer in the brain, as cocaine does.

The nicotine stays attached to the receptors much longer than acetylcholine does, taking up the space. The brain compensates by producing more acetylcholine and growing more acetylcholine receptors. When a smoker first stops smoking, there is too much acetycholine in the brain creating extreme nervousness. It takes one to two weeks for the acetycholine levels and receptors to return to normal after a smoker stops smoking.

The nicotine reaches its peak before the cigarette is finished and stays in the system about 30 minutes. At that point, the craving returns with the beginning symptoms of withdrawal. The drop in glucose that happens at this time results in depression and fatigue, causing a hypoglycemic effect and the increased acetylcholine creates anxiety. The cycle goes something like this, per cigarette:

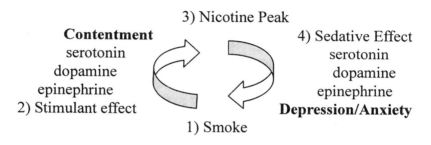

The stress hormone corticosterone reduces the effect of nicotine and more nicotine is needed for the same effect. The receptors shrink and become desensitized. The smoker develops an increased tolerance to nicotine and this increases the addiction. The production of stress hormones being shut on and off as withdrawal starts and stops results in a hypersensitive system where stress chemicals are released at the slightest provocation (sensitization) triggering the need for another smoke (74).

Women are at Greater Risk

Women are more likely to develop lung cancer than men even if they smoke fewer cigarettes. The risk of lung cancer is nearly double in women who smoke compared to men who smoke (64). Female smokers are two to six times more likely to have a heart attack than men who smoke. The risk is even greater for heart disease and stroke if a women who smokes is taking oral contraceptives. Smoking is also a contributing factor to osteoporosis as it reduces bone mineral density (49).

It can be more difficult for women to stop smoking. Women are generally more concerned about weight gain than men who stop smoking (62). Women are also more susceptible to the triggers (anchors) to smoke such as associating smoking with specific moods, people, places and things (64).

Cigarette Smoking – A Major Factor in Infertility for Men and Women

If you are trying to get pregnant and you or your partner smoke cigarettes, you may want to know that smoking decreases fertility by about 50% in both men and women (49, 54)). Here's how: Female smokers have a decrease in ovulation and there is a less likely chance a fertilized egg will implant (49). Nicotine also interferes with the function of the fallopian tubes and can result in tubal pregnancies. Smoking decreases the function of the ovaries, including estrogen, and increases the early onset of menopause (36).

The risk of miscarriage is increased by about 39% in female smokers (49). There is also a higher incident of stillborn births. The risk of Sudden Infant Death Syndrome is three times higher for babies exposed to tobacco smoke (49).

Cadium, the poisonous battery metal that's in cigarettes, is a factor in the male smoker's decrease in fertility and damage to the sperm, as well as a reduction in the sperm count, sperm density, and the proportion of mobile sperm (54). There is also a decrease in testosterone in male smokers. Damaged sperm can result in birth abnormalities. The damage to the sperm can affect future generations through the abnormalities and effects on DNA (54).

If you or your partner are smokers and you want to get pregnant, it is suggested that you both stop smoking at least four months before pregnancy to produce a healthy egg and sperm, and ultimately a healthy baby (54).

Effects on an Unborn Child

There are levels of cadium in the amniotic fluid of a mother who smokes during pregnancy. This interferes with the metabolism of zinc and affects birth weight. Babies born to mothers who smoke during pregnancy often have a lower birth weight, and a smaller head circumference (54).

Cadium can also reduce the placenta's blood flow to the baby during development. The levels of carbon monoxide are twice as high in the developing fetus as they are in the smoking mother (48). This decreases the oxygen supply to the baby. When a mother smokes during pregnancy there is a reduction in cell replication in the developing fetus affecting all the developing organs. This damage is usually most significant in the first few weeks of pregnancy. Smoking during pregnancy increases the risk of birth defects by 29% (54).

Reduced brain weight and reduced thickness of the cerebral cortex is associated with babies born to mothers who smoke during pregnancy. There is a decrease in the dendrite branching that makes the connections to other brain cells (48). These connections are what physically happen in the brain when learning occurs.

A mother smoking during pregnancy significantly increases the risk that the child will have problems with hyperactivity, problems paying attention, learning and behavioral problems, as well as scoring lower on I.Q. tests (48, 54). The higher the doses of nicotine used during pregnancy, the more damaging the effects on the child.

There is a correlation between an increase in female smokers and an increase in ADHD in children over the last thirty years. Long range follow up studies showed that children of mothers who smoked during pregnancy continued to have more health and academic problems. They also had a 50% higher risk of being admitted to the hospital for asthma and had more respiratory problems in general (48).

Babies who are breast fed by mothers who smoke are fed the same toxins found in cigarettes through the breast milk, and smoking decreases breast milk production.

Effects of Second Hand Smoke on Children

Children that are exposed to environmental smoke, also known as second hand smoke, performed more poorly than smoke-free children on I.Q. tests during research studies (48). Children of active smokers had problems with misbehavior, were more active, and had more problems with school adjustment.

The harmful chemicals that are in cigarettes are also present in environmental smoke. They not only go into the lungs and bloodstream of the smoker, but the same effects happen to anyone exposed to the smoke, including children and pets. Environmental smoke can disrupt the central nervous system of children exposed to it.

The toxic substances in cigarettes are carried into the bloodstream not just into the lungs. Carbon monoxide attaches to the hemoglobin that carries oxygen through the bloodstream and changes about 10% of the hemoglobin to carboxyhemoglobin. This means the oxygen level is reduced and carbon monoxide travels throughout the body (53).

Children exposed to environmental smoke experience this the same as the smoker does. This carbon monoxide effect is associated with the shortness of breath smokers often experience and the respiratory problems children exposed to smoke frequently have.

Your denial system may tell you that if you smoke in another room from your child they are safe. Smoke does not stay confined to one area in a home. It travels through the ventilation system in your home and goes everywhere air goes. It takes two weeks for nicotine to clear a room after the last cigarette (51).

Children exposed to environmental smoke experience more colds, influenza and ear infections. There are 10 million children under the age of six regularly exposed to environmental smoke and approximately 50,000 people die each year in the USA due to environmental smoke exposure (58).

Cancer in All of Us?

One of the most damaging effects of cigarette smoke on the smoker and those exposed to smoke is a compromised immune system. Studies indicate we all have cancer cells in our body, but our immune system gets rid of them before it becomes significant enough to do us serious harm (15, 18). Smoking depletes several important vitamins in the body including antioxidants like vitamin A, C and E, and vitamin B6, magnesium and chromium.

Macrophages are our systems answer to cleaning out toxins, bacteria, dirt and any other substances that threatens the balance of our system. They act as little "Pac Men" eating the debris. Smokers have about ten times more macrophages than non-smokers. This is due to the torrent of toxins cigarette smoke pours into the body. More macrophages are produced to do the clean up job. Unfortunately, as more and more macrophages are produced and taxed past their limit, a mutation of their own cells occurs. The macrophages become cancerous and spread throughout the body. This is known as small cell lung cancer (15).

Withdrawal – The Flip Side of the Coin

When a smoker goes through withdrawal the brain's pleasure systems go through dramatic changes in the same way that withdrawal from cocaine, opiates, amphetamines and alcohol happens.

In a research study, rats were given nicotine for one week. For up to two weeks after discontinuing the nicotine, their brains showed a 40% decrease in response to pleasure due to the reduction or shrinking of dopamine receptors from the nicotine use (59). When you use a substance to trigger the pleasure systems of your brain, regardless of whether that substance is sugar, caffeine, nicotine, alcohol, heroin, cocaine or any other addictive substance, you diminish your body's natural production of those pleasure chemicals.

Your own "manufacturing plant" can shut down or be altered as a result of chronic substance abuse. There is a decrease in ability to feel pleasure that lasts several days, and there is a strong sense of anxiety and depression if the withdrawal happens suddenly. The effects of withdrawal can also include anger and aggression. The need to get relief from these symptoms can lead to relapse. The ability to feel pleasure returns as your brain replenishes its dopamine receptors after continued abstinence of nicotine.

Here's some good news. Nicotine and carbon monoxide levels are reduced by 50% within 8 hours after the last cigarette. By 24 hours, the carbon monoxide is eliminated. Within 48 hours there is no nicotine left in the body. Within 72 hours breathing begins to improve (46).

A gradual reduction in nicotine through the withdrawal period can help reduce the withdrawal effects. There are several products on the market that assist in gradual withdrawal from nicotine. Using nicotine replacement products approximately doubles your chance of successfully quitting (46). The physical symptoms of withdrawal can last two to three weeks, and the chance of relapse decreases after about three months.

Bupropion is a medication used to help smokers stop smoking. It is a prescription medication sold under the trade name of Zyban. The antidepressant medication, Wellbutrin, is also bupropion.

Research is close to finding effective treatment that can block the effects of nicotine, thus eliminating nicotine's addictive quality (50). A chemical that blocks the effects of another chemical is called an antagonist. This blocking of the pleasurable effects means there would be no chemical release "payoff" for smoking.

A vaccine that acts as an antagonist for nicotine is being developed and clinical trials are scheduled to start in 2002. Topiramate, sold under the brand name Topamax, is a new drug used for the treatment of epilepsy that shows promise as an antagonist to block the effects of nicotine.

Nicotine use stimulates two different neurotransmitter pathways that activate the release of not only dopamine, but norepinephrine and serotonin as well. When used in a research study on rats at the U.S. Department of Energy's Brookhaven National Laboratory, topiramate blocked the increases in norepinephrine and dopamine triggered by nicotine, and *increased* serotonin.

In other human studies, an increase in serotonin has been shown to decrease the incidence of smoking (63). Estrogen also increases serotonin. While we are waiting for the miracles of science, let's look at some techniques that can benefit you right now.

Why You Haven't Quit

The techniques offered here are tools that may be used in conjunction with established existing modes of treatment. It is not suggested that the following techniques are all anyone needs to overcome an addiction problem. No single treatment technique works for all people. The greater the treatment options, the better the chance someone will find something(s) that works for them.

Treatment of substance abuse and addiction is a life and death matter that requires very specific and specialized treatment. Support groups such as Alcoholics Anonymous (AA) and Narcotics Anonymous (NA) are lifelines to those seeking help with their addictions.

Many people feel their lives have been saved by their involvement in these programs, and many unselfish and caring people dedicate their lives as sponsors to help others who are where they have been. Support groups are also available to family members through Alanon and Alateen.

Giving up smoking can't be easy. If it were, there wouldn't be so many people vacillating between going to great lengths to stop, and continuing to smoke while denying it may very well kill them. Mark Twain is quoted as saying, "Giving up smoking is easy. I do it every day." (14)

What is the advantage of smoking? What is the payoff, and how can the reward be so worth the punishment? Our own built in pleasure system is the jackpot of payoffs in substance addiction. The same pleasure systems are activated whether you are addicted to cigarettes or cocaine. Like most people who delve into risk-taking behavior, smokers take the risk telling themselves they will be in that small percentage that doesn't die early from smoking (and ignore their compromised health).

There are some payoffs that seem worth the risk. Millions of people spend a dollar, or more, to buy a lottery ticket that could be worth millions. Even though we know how slim the odds of winning are, we buy them anyway because the potential payoff is greater than the low risk of a few dollars. This is not to minimize gambling addictions that can be as equally damaging to lives as substance addictions.

There is a certain amount of risk in a business venture, making a decision about a career move, or a possible geographic relocation. In these situations you are in control. You are making a rational choice after carefully considering your options.

With substance addiction, however, there is something added

to the mix. You have no control. The essence of substance addiction is the lack of control. If you have control, you are not addicted. But, denial is also a fundamental element in substance addiction.

Many people who are addicted to a substance deny they have lost control, or if they have that awareness, they minimize it. If you are not sure whether or not you are addicted to a particular substance, the quickest and easiest way to find out is to stop using that substance. You will know within a short period of time whether you have control or the substance does.

If you are a smoker or have other substance addictions, no one needs to tell you what happens when you stop smoking, drinking alcohol or using your substance of choice. You probably know first hand. You most likely have tried to quit more than once.

Cognitively you know the risks, but the instant gratification of the reward is, at least temporarily, worth the punishment. The ultimate and greater punishment of the effects on those you love, poor health, and possible death get buried in the darkness of denial.

The need for internal physical and emotional equilibrium takes over, and is punctuated by the strong craving you feel when you go too long without a cigarette or other addictive substance.

Your belief system is at the helm. In *Phantoms in the Brain*, V.S. Ramachandran and Sandra Blakeslee state that the coping strategies of the two hemispheres of the brain are different. "The left hemisphere's job is to create a belief system or model to fold new experiences into that belief system. If confronted with some new information that doesn't fit the model, it relies on Freudian defense mechanisms to deny, repress, or confabulate —anything to preserve the status quo."

The right hemisphere questions and considers change. The left hemisphere doesn't want to change. So what is the deciding factor in our dueling brains? As you know, the answer is endorphins, dopamine and the rest. The scale is then tilted.

Studies show that heavy alcohol drinkers have high levels of endorphins in their blood but lower levels in their spinal fluid, indicating their natural state is deficient in endorphins (10). Many people use substances to self medicate a brain chemistry that may be prone to depression, anxiety or other mental health problems. Nicotine, caffeine and food are often used to neutralize feelings of depression and anxiety rather than seeking treatment for these problems.

Alcohol addiction decreases life expectancy by approximately 10-15 years. That's if you are not killed in another manner related to alcohol abuse. Drunk drivers are responsible for approximately half of all fatal automobile accidents (71). Alcohol kills brain cells and damages every organ in the body. With chronic use, alcohol interferes with the digestive system preventing the absorption of fat and proteins, and decreases the absorption of vitamins A, D, E and K. With long-term alcohol abuse, the body becomes unable to absorb vitamin B-1 (thiamine) resulting in brain damage that effects cognitive functioning.

Alcohol, as with cigarettes, affects women greater than men. Women are less able to break down alcohol so more is absorbed into the bloodstream (71). A woman's sexual desire and menstruation cycle can be affected by alcohol abuse, and about 40,000 children are born each year with birth defects as a result of women drinking alcohol during pregnancy (68).

There is a narcotic antagonist (pleasure blocker) called Naltrexone approved by the FDA for use in the treatment of alcoholism. It is not a magic bullet, but can be used with other modes of treatment. An antagonist for marijuana has been discovered in Paris, France by Sanofi-Synthelabo. Studies to further test this antagonist are presently underway in the United States as well (75).

Maintaining your physical sense of well being, as well as

working within your existing patterns and associations, increases your opportunity for success. If changes are not congruent with your belief system, they may not be lasting.

The following questionnaire is designed to assist you in examining your associations and patterns with smoking or other substance use.

Assessing Childhood Patterns/Associations That Keep You Hooked

1. How old were you when you started smoking/drinking/using? What were the circumstances?

2. Does anyone else in your family smoke/drink/use, if so who: What are your "family traditions" regarding substance use/abuse/addiction?

3. What are your beliefs about smoking/drinking/using?

4. What areas of your life are currently, or in the past, being affected by your smoking/drinking/using (i.e. relationships, job, health, legal, etc.)?

5. How has your smoking/drinking/using affected others in your life? If you don't know, ask them.

6. What are your expectations about how your smoking/drinking/using will affect your life, and those you love, in the future?

7. Has any close family member or friend become seriously ill or died as a result of smoking/drinking/using? If so who? How did this affect you?

8. Do you have health risks that can worsen if you continue to smoke/drink use? What are they?

9. Specifically when do you smoke/drink/use? What is your routine or habits? (i.e. morning, after a meal or sex, alone or with friends?)

10. What triggers you to smoke/drink/use more frequently than you normally do?

11. How do you feel emotionally and physically when you have not been able to smoke/drink/use for a prolonged period of time?

12. List all associations you make with cigarettes, alcohol, or other substance of choice until you can't think of any more.

13. What would you lose if you gave up smoking/drinking/using?

14. I don't want to stop smoking/drinking/using because:

15. What would you gain if you gave up smoking, drinking, using?

16. I want to stop smoking/drinking/using because:

After you have explored your patterns, associations and beliefs regarding smoking/drinking/using, use this information to design your own individual stop smoking/drinking/using strategies that will work for you. Using the *Developing Your Super Powers Workbook* will help you do this. Since each individual's answers to the above questions will be different, where and specifically how you make changes and work within your patterns will come from you. Here are some suggestions that might help you get started.

Consider the generational patterns in your family. Is there someone in your family that you relate to primarily through your common addiction(s)? Maybe it is a spouse or partner. You may feel you would have very little connection to this person if you didn't smoke, drink, or use together, and this relationship is important to you. If you decide giving up your addiction is also important to you, how do you resolve this conflict?

If you look closely, you will probably find other common interests with this person. The other interests may not be as strong as the addiction link, but they could be strengthened. You can build new interests together, if the other person is willing. Depending on the type of addiction and level of addiction, you may find that being around others with the same problem is detrimental to your own recovery and you need to limit contact. This can be difficult to do.

Think of substance addiction as kryptonite that is not only draining your Super Powers, but your more basic abilities and your health as well. Kryptonite is the only substance that can weaken Superman and it comes from pieces of Superman's home planet, Krypton. Krypton blew up when Superman was a child. Before the explosion, his parents sent him to earth to save him. Are there pieces from your childhood that act as your kryptonite? If so, what are they?

The first step is developing an awareness of the patterns. Sometimes awareness alone points you in the right direction and your subconscious mind will follow, giving you the answers instinctively, and helping you stay on track.

Knowing your triggers to smoke/drink/use more frequently is another area where you can work within your existing associations and patterns for success. Observe yourself for a few days. Know your routine and identify when you smoke/drink/

use more often. Stress and feelings of anxiety are common triggers for smoking or use of other substances.

If you smoke to decrease stress or anxiety and you associate smoking with drinking coffee or some other form of caffeine there is a paradox. When you drink coffee you trigger a release of adrenaline, which makes you anxious and triggers a need to smoke so you can calm down. You have your cigarette with coffee and around and around you go. It does more than that, however.

In her book *Molecules of Emotion,* Candace Pert states, "Each of us has his or her own natural pharmacopoeia — the very finest drugstore available at the cheapest cost — to produce all the drugs we ever need to run our bodymind in precisely the way it was designed to run over centuries of evolution."

She uses overuse of sugar to make this point. The body naturally produces glucose (sugar), which is the brain's fuel. Our liver regulates this function. Excessive sugar intake results in flooding and desensitizing the receptors and interfering in the body's natural process of producing and utilizing glucose. This same flooding and desensitizing of receptors happens if we take in excessive amounts of caffeine or excessive amounts of any substance.

Stress steroids are released with both caffeine and nicotine use and they depress the immune system leaving us susceptible to illness. People who are depressed also have high levels of stress steroids.

The body naturally produces a chemical called adenosine to help us relax and go to sleep. Caffeine is referred to as an "antiadenosine". Caffeine shuts off the adenosine receptors with just one cup of coffee. Studies show that excessive caffeine use results in the brain growing more adenosine receptors in the brain's attempt to self-adjust.

The result is a need to consume more and more caffeine for equal or the same results, even further throwing the body out of its natural order. The more caffeine we drink the more we need to drink to stay awake. This overuse of caffeine also results in the withdrawal symptoms of excessive drowsiness, headaches and caffeine craving when we initially stop using it (10).

If you associate nicotine with caffeine, reducing or eliminating caffeine may help you stop smoking. The aversion technique described in Chapter 6 can help you eliminate caffeine.

Once you identify the triggers for your favorite "poison", develop a list of antidotes, giving yourself many alternative ways to choose your brain chemistry naturally to overcome your addiction(s). Knowing what brain chemistry "cocktail" you are seeking can help you identify triggers and develop alternatives. Do you smoke/drink/use to ease depression or anxiety? Do you smoke/drink/use for excitement, possibly as a cure for boredom? Do you smoke/drink/use to feel a sense of belonging or connectedness to others? Do you smoke/drink/use to calm down and relax? There is a specific brain chemistry combination with each of these desired states of mind and more than one way to achieve them.

If your desired state is calm, for example, feed yourself sensory experiences that elicit a sense of calm. You can trigger your stored memories of calm. Anchors for calm may include music as auditory anchors, massage and warm baths as touch anchors, and positive self-talk as verbal anchors. Each of these anchor associations can change your brain chemistry from anxiety to calm.

The process of meditation is used to feel calm and relaxed and get in touch with your subconscious mind. Transcendental Meditation has been used successfully to reduce or eliminate substance abuse.

If you are seeking a state of mind that includes a rush of adrenaline, expand your experiences to include activities that will give you this brain chemistry state without using harmful substances. Physical activity increases endorphins and can release adrenaline.

People continue negative patterns of behavior out of conditioning and secondary gains. Working to reshape and change what reinforces this behavior while working within your established associations and patterns will give you optimal opportunities for success.

Make a mental or written list of what works for you. Give yourself a smorgasbord of sensory anchors to choose from since not all of them can work in every setting. You can also access PMOs to trigger some of those same pleasure chemicals naturally.

When you get through the physical withdrawal (about 2–3 weeks), that gnawing craving diminishes. Adding quality and years to your life for two or three weeks of withdrawal is not a bad tradeoff. But that's a left hemisphere thought. For the right hemisphere, accessing your own pleasure chemicals can make the withdrawal period easier to get through. More people will be successful in overcoming their addictions if it is not so emotionally or physically painful to quit.

Here are some other techniques that may help you stop smoking or using addictive substances.

Super Power Techniques to Stop Smoking

1. Accenting the Negative

This technique is the form of aversion therapy described in Chapter 6 that helps you give up unhealthy food or drinks. It is based on associating a negative smell and taste with the particular substance you want to stop using. Addictive substances trick our pleasure/pain systems into thinking our body is getting something good for us. After all, we are wired so that we get pleasure when we do something that will preserve our life and species. So, if we get a rush of pleasure when we smoke cigarettes, shoot heroine, abuse alcohol, or inhale cocaine, our body thinks we are getting something that will keep us ticking longer. We may know intellectually that this is not true, even through our denial, but physiologically we are getting the opposite message.

While you are waiting for science to develop that effective antagonist or "blocker" of pleasure received from substance use, you can intervene now and create your own antagonist by associating a negative taste and smell with your addictive substance when you use it. This will neutralize the pleasurable effect of this substance and assist you in quitting.

If you want to use this technique to stop smoking, choose something that has a smell and taste that is particularly distasteful to you. It needs to be something you can smell and put in your mouth without being harmful. Something liquid may be easier to use.

Make a commitment to yourself that you can smoke all the cigarettes you want (like it so far?), but, before you take the first puff, you will put a drop of the negative tasting stuff of choice on your tongue, and take a big whiff of it. You don't have to put it on your tongue more than once, unless you want to, but breath in the negative smell before each puff you take.

You need to place some of your chosen negative taste/smell stuff in a small container and have it available wherever you go. You might soak cotton swabs in it and carry those in a sealed container. Consistency is essential to success. The associations are generally made very quickly.

This technique is working within the right hemisphere of your brain where your sensory input is processed and where your pleasure systems lie. The association of the negative taste and smell with cigarette smoking interferes with the pleasure you normally derive from cigarettes. Smoking isn't experienced in the same way after you make the negative associations. Your brain is given mixed signals. If the negative signal becomes stronger than the positive signal you may find picking up another cigarette, or other substance, one of the last things you want to do.

Here is a personal example of how this works. On my sister's third birthday, our mother baked her a pineapple upside down cake. My sister decided to salt it before eating it, a typical three-year-old thing to do. Before anyone could stop her, she accidentally dumped the whole box of salt on the cake. We tried to resurrect the cake, but somehow it didn't taste as good with a box of salt on top, even when we dusted it off. After a couple of bites, we threw it into the trashcan. The negative outweighed the positive.

Once the negative associations are made, all you need to do is think of smoking a cigarette and the negative smell and taste will also appear and you will likely decide to pass.

2. Ordeal Technique

A technique similar to the negative associations described above is one used in Ordeal Therapy. It is based on the same principle of associating something negative with a behavior or habit you wish to stop. Choose a task(s) that you do not enjoy and contract with yourself to complete this task before you can have a cigarette. What the tasks are will be individual, of course, and whether you are at home, work or out socially will be a factor. Chores you find unpleasant or physical activity you don't enjoy are ordeal tasks you may want to incorporate into your plan. The idea is to make smoking, or other substance use, an ordeal rather than a pleasure, and delay tactics can help you gradually reduce your nicotine intake as you work towards your goal to quit.

3. Non-dominate Hand Technique to Stop Smoking

This technique also works to offset the side of your dueling brain hemisphere that is winning when you continue to smoke and you want to stop. You might try it in conjunction with the aversion technique, or by itself. It is very simple. The next time you smoke a cigarette, hold it in your non-dominant hand and do not switch it to your dominant hand.

Think of how you feel when you try to write with your non-dominant hand. This usually takes more effort and concentration and feels awkward and uncomfortable. There is a strong need to switch back to what is comfortable, unless you are one of the few people who can use both hands equally.

The point is to make smoking awkward and bring each time you hold a cigarette into your conscious awareness by using your non-dominant hand. Basically, you give more thought to what you are doing. It can shed a little light in the "denial corners" of your brain regarding just how much you smoke. It may also help you cut down on the number of cigarettes you are smoking while you are working on stopping since you would not be smoking absent-mindedly.

4. Imagery Exercises to Stop Smoking

The following is an imagery exercise to help you stop smoking. It can be modified to fit your individual circumstances. The example given is written for a smoker with a young child or children. If this doesn't fit you, any significant person in your life can be used in the imagery. It is designed to help someone stop smoking, but it can be used for any other substance abuse or addiction. This imagery exercise can be emotionally powerful and, I will give you warning, it is designed to filtrate the denial system. All you need to do is get comfortable, relax and simply read it. After you make the modifications to fit you, reread it or have someone read it to you. There are also CD's and audiotapes available (order information in back of book).

Imagery Exercise #1:

Each and every time I pick up a cigarette and before I light it, in my mind's eye, I will see very clearly and distinctly my beautiful child picking up a cigarette ready to light one also.

She watches everything I do. I am her best teacher. As I light my cigarette, I will see myself instructing my child how to hold her cigarette so it doesn't fall and how to hold the lighter so she doesn't get burned. I am very protective of my child. After I light my cigarette, my child will light hers and I will see the smoke billowing around her head. I know what is in that smoke. She will cough at first, but she will get used to it. She's used to my smoke. She is excited at doing such a "grown up" thing and thinks her friends will be impressed.

I inhale again, and so does she. She gets a pleasant smile on her face and can't wait for the next puff. Smoke continues to swirl around both our heads and into our bodies. It clings to our skin, clothes and hair and attaches itself to everything in the room. She watches me intently and inhales each and every time I do, until the cigarette is gone and we each put out our cigarette.

I give my child a hug. I love her so much. I would give my life for her.

Fast forward to the future. Maybe it is several years from now, or maybe it is tomorrow.

I see myself in the doctor's office being told I have cancer and will have to go through chemotherapy and radiation. It doesn't work. Nothing works.

My daughter is scared I am going to leave her forever. She asks in desperation, "But, what about my graduation?" Her mind races ahead. " What about my wedding? Who will be the grandmother to my children? Mom, how can I live without you?"

But she has to. She is sad and angry and hurt. She visits the cemetery often and puts beautiful flowers on my grave. She cries and cries, and as she walks away she pulls out her cigarettes because she really needs one right now.

Suddenly I wake up. It was all a dream. My relief is immediate. I have a feeling much like someone would if they could see a newspaper from the future that described her death in a terrible accident on a certain date. I hear the warning. I can change the circumstances and avoid the tragedy. I have a deeper awareness of the beauty and gift of life, and I vow to never let this awakening slip away from me.

I make the changes now.

Imagery Exercise #2:

This next imagery exercise is not designed to address your denial system or your emotions. This imagery exercise is similar to those used in self-healing. It can be used anytime, but, for extra benefit, try it just before going to sleep at night. Using it at that time can help you access your subconscious for greater results.

Get comfortable and relaxed. Close your eyes if that is comfortable for you. Take at least three slow deep breaths through your nose and out your mouth, inhaling and exhaling deeply. Take as many deep breaths as you need in through your nose, and out through your mouth until you begin to feel a sense of calm.

When you feel yourself begin to relax, pay attention to how the air going into and out of your lungs feels. If you have any difficulty with breathing, this will subside as you continue to take deeper breaths and relax more and more. The oxygen you are breathing in is going exactly where it needs to go. Your breathing takes on a natural rhythm that is in sync with your heartbeat.

You become more aware of this soft methodical rhythm as you continue to breath deeply in and out. You can hear the air going in and out smoothly. Your lungs are healthy and strong and cooperate fully with your breathing process.

As you continue to breathe in and out deeply and easily, you continue to be soothed by your body's natural rhythm. You send messages to your body that goes everywhere the oxygen travels.

You make a promise to yourself and your body that you will no longer purposefully put anything into it that will cause your body to be harmed. You give your body the message that it is healthy and strong. You send the message to your lungs to become pink and healthy. Each time you breathe out you are releasing the toxic chemicals and other harmful substances in your lungs and blood stream out of your body. Your lungs are grateful and cooperate fully with your breathing process. They believe your promise.

What If You Don't Want to Stop?

In his informative and inspirational book *Love, Medicine and Miracles,* Dr. Bernie Siegel writes, "Part of the mind's effect on health is direct and conscious. The extent to which we love ourselves determines whether we eat right, get enough sleep, smoke, wear seat belts, exercise and so on. Each of these choices is a statement of how much we care about living. These decisions control about 90% of the factors that determines our health. The trouble is that most people's motivation to attend to these basics is deflected by attitudes hidden from every day awareness. As a result, many of us have mixed intentions." What are your "hidden attitudes" that result in not taking care of yourself?

Transactional Analysis (TA) is a form of psychotherapy

founded by Dr. Eric Berne that was very big in the 1970's and continues to be used worldwide. A concept in TA is called life scripts. A life script reflects a person's beliefs, either consciously or subconsciously, about themselves, and the direction he or she expects his or her life to take.

Direct and indirect messages we are given in childhood, our role in the family, and others' beliefs about us that we instinctively knew, even if they were never directly stated, all influence our life scripts. These parental messages may range from a belief that a child is special and they are really going to make their mark someday, to a belief that "this child should've never been born."

As children, we internalize these messages and learn what others' expectations are for us. More often than not, we live up or down to these expectations, as the case may be. There can be a significant incident or event in your life that impacts you so emotionally that almost everything else you do is based on the belief you carry away with you.

Often we receive conflicting messages about ourselves. One significant person in our lives may have had high expectations of us while another did not. Who do we believe? This can result in a lifetime of inner conflict. We may have starts and stops in many directions but never get anywhere. We may also find ourselves with this pattern if the basic life script we carried with us from childhood is negative and we have challenged it, but we haven't gone far enough to overcome these negative beliefs at present. Our life scripts directly impact the choices we make and how we treat ourselves.

Abuse and neglect is often thought of as happening to children or battered women. There are many forms of abuse and neglect that we inflict upon ourselves, much of it without realizing the impact. We may not realize how our life script is directing us, or at least, adding ambiguity to our lives.

The following is a list of some of the ways we sometimes

abuse and neglect ourselves. There are surely others.

Indicators of Self-Neglect

WHEN YOU DON'T –

> Go to the doctor when you are ill, or follow up with important medical advice
>
> Go to the doctor for preventive annual check ups
>
> Go to the dentist for check ups and needed dental work
>
> Eat healthy
>
> Go for regular eye exams and keep your contact or glasses prescription updated
>
> Stay physically active
>
> Pay attention to your basic physical needs for rest, food, clothing, etc.
>
> Work reasonable hours
>
> Get enough fun time or enrichment experiences
>
> Use your talents
>
> Get in touch with your spirituality

Indicators of Self-Abuse

WHEN YOU –

    Smoke cigarettes

    Abuse alcohol or other addictive substances

    Abuse prescription medications

    Disregard your own safety

    Continue in relationships with people who abuse you

    Do anything to physically harm your self

    Gamble excessively

    Drive under the influence of alcohol or any substance, prescribed or otherwise

    Abuse others

    Spend excessively

These are just some of the ways we can be self-abusive and self-neglectful. It is not implied that all medical neglect is a choice. Certainly there is not an equal distribution of wealth, resources or medical care available to everyone. There are designated government funds for those needing medical/dental/prescription and eye care services that cannot afford to pay for them, but the system has a wide gap that many hard working people fall into. For many, even providing for the basic needs of their families and themselves can be trying.

There are also those who have the medical coverage who don't use it when they need it. For many people it is a matter of prioritizing. There are ways to be good to yourself and show self-love whether you have money or not. If you don't feel a sense of self-love, you might ask, "How do I do that?"

Self-love does not equal selfishness. They are two different things. Some very selfish people can be the most self-abusing and self-neglectful of all. Just as we establish patterns of behavior with food and substances, the patterns and associations we have about our own self-worth is the underpin for everything else we do.

What is your life script? Are you willing to continue living it out? Life scripts can be changed. You are affected by others' beliefs about you when you are an adult just as you are as a child.

If you find yourself surrounded by people who convey negative messages about you, know that you don't have to accept it. Set healthy boundaries for yourself. It is as equally important to listen to yourself and what messages you are giving others. Frequently, if we are not very happy with ourselves, we tend to be critical of others.

A place to start with improving self-critical behavior or thoughts is to develop an awareness of how we treat other people, as well as how we treat ourselves. Choose your natural brain chemistry that will give you the outcome you are looking for. You can start on the inside by self-correcting negative thoughts and actions, or on the outside with noticing how you treat others and modifying critical behavior. Either way, you benefit, and so do those around you.

If you don't *feel* love for yourself, pretend you do. Take inventory of any self-abusive and self-neglectful behaviors and work on changing them whether you feel self-love or not. Pretend you love yourself and treat yourself as well as you treat those you love, until it becomes real.

Choosing Happiness

Do you find that you have particular moods or feelings that dominate your other feelings? Some people walk around with a predominate mood of anger. Others may feel worried and anxious most of the time. A predominant feeling of sadness can have devastating effects on someone's life and health.

We develop neurological patterns of moods and feelings just as we do behaviors. Neurological pathways deepen and become lightening fast through repetitive actions (behaviors). Learned behaviors are accompanied with thoughts and feelings. We learn behaviors and we learn emotional responses. We go to the deepest and most familiar basin with mood as we do with anything else. The deeper the neurological "groove", the quicker we go there, whether we want to or not.

A child who witnesses ongoing domestic violence may learn to be angry and aggressive or fearful and intimated. Either way, it is likely they will recreate circumstances in their adult lives that will keep these old feelings alive and thriving.

Think about your feelings as a child. A child overwhelmed with adult responsibility very often becomes an overly responsible adult who creates circumstances that continue those familiar feelings in the present. Children who grow up feeling unloved or invisible may find themselves feeling the same much of their adult lives. They may "filter out" anyone who contradicts their core belief that they are unlovable, and maintain relationships that validate their limiting belief.

These neurological pathways are engraved, but they are not engraved in stone. Computers are built to store and retrieve memory, and to perform specific functions they have been programmed to carry out. Computer programs can be changed. The human brain is not a computer. After all, there is a human person and human spirit attached. However, neurological wiring is much like electrical wiring and it has electrical energy. The human brain is more highly advanced than any computer in existence and the human spirit gives us more power than any machine could ever have. We can change our "pre-programming" with recognition of what we want to change, the desire to change it, and the know how to go about it.

If your predominant mood is not happy and happy is how you would like to feel, you can learn to choose happiness. Here are some steps to help you change a predominantly negative mood.

1. Identify your predominant moods. At first, just note when you are in one of these moods without trying to change it.

2. Look for the triggers and patterns associated with your predominant moods. When was the earliest time you remember feeling this way? What childhood patterns are you recreating today?

3. Pay very close attention to how you feel physically and emotionally when you are happy. What does your brain chemical "cocktail" of happiness feel like in your head and body? Commit these brain and body experiences to memory.

4. Anchor this feeling and practice recalling feelings of happiness.

5. Identify your triggers for *happiness* and do more of those activities/behaviors. This deepens your "happiness" basin. **Give yourself permission to feel happy.**

6. When one of your less desirable predominant moods reappears, use self-talk in whatever words fit you to say,

"There it is again." Learn to recognize it.

7. Mentally release the negative mood and use your happiness anchors to recall the desired state of happiness.

There are predominant moods that can be life threatening. If you are chronically depressed or have any suicidal ideations, get help immediately. In an advice column several years ago I read this statement, "Suicide is a permanent solution to a temporary problem." Most people who contemplate suicide don't want to end their lives. They want to end their pain. Clinical depression can be successfully treated.

When your mood changes your brain chemistry changes. As you become more skilled at choosing your own brain chemistry naturally, the easier it becomes to choose your mood.

Anger Control Technique

If you have a problem with anger control, here is an imagery exercise to help you change that neurological wiring that takes you to a place of anger quickly.

Visualize your anger as the red line of mercury on a thermometer that rises as your temperature goes up. Take your baseline "temperature". What degree is the red line on when you are calm and not feeling angry? Memorize your brain chemistry "cocktail" for calm. Give it a number. This is your calm state "temperature." Take your "temperature" again when you are angry, and your varying degree of anger. What are those numbers?

Your baseline calm "temperature" can be an inner visual anchor that you use to return to calm. If the highest degree on the thermometer is 100, and your calm state "temperature" is 25, then your goal is to return to 25 or below. Identify the physical changes in your body when you are angry and learn to read the signals *before* the mercury gets high. Visualize the number gradually decreasing and the red line dropping as you regain your composure.

You can learn to change your mood to a more positive one as quickly as your old negative moods previously appeared. Be creative and come up with your own mind strategies that work for you.

Chapter Nine

BEYOND THE PHYSICAL

*The secret of making something
work in our lives is, first of all,
the deep desire to make it work:
then the faith and belief
that it can work:
then to hold that clear definite vision
in your consciousness and
see it working step by step,
without one thought of doubt or disbelief.*

Eileen Caddy

Creating Your Own Time Machine

Transcendental Meditation (TM) is a form of meditation originating in the Eastern regions of our world. Some of the benefits of TM include increasing intelligence and creativity, improving memory and reaction time, reducing stress and anxiety, promoting self-healing and increasing longevity.
    Transcendental Mediation can be used to bring mechanical body functions into conscious awareness and control functions regulated by the primitive parts of the brain. Simply with thought,

meditation can be used to lower heart rate and blood pressure, lower or raise body temperature in a chosen area, stop the flow of blood, control irregular heart beat and reduce pain, to name a few.

People who meditate regularly show evidence of having a much younger physiological and psychological age than their chronological age, by as much as 5 – 12 years (5).

In his book *Ageless Body Timeless Mind,* Dr. Deepak Chopra describes an experiment conducted in 1979 by a psychologist, Ellen Langer, and her colleagues at Harvard University. A research study included taking a group of men 75 years old and older to a resort for a week. Half of the men in the study were told to pretend the year was 1959 and act accordingly. All of their discussions had to be within that context. The resort was decorated to look as though it were 1959. Great care was taken, down to the most finite detail, to give the feel and image of the year 1959.

The other half of the group acted as a control group. These men simply had a week at the resort without the 1959 experience. All the men were given physical tests to determine their biological age before the experiment. They were tested again after their week at the resort. The results were remarkable.

The men who pretended the year was 1959 showed very measurable physiological changes. They were more flexible and had better muscle strength. Their hearing and vision improved. They had less stiffening of the joints and their fingers even lengthened. They also looked visibly younger. All this was after only one week of simply thinking of themselves as twenty years younger and acting accordingly. They accessed their memories of those times and literally turned back time in their minds and bodies. The tangible anchors (1959 props) aided them in this transition.

The music that was played during this experiment was, of course, only music from the year 1959. When we hear a song that we associate with a particular experience from the past, our brain chemistry replicates the brain chemistry we had when we heard the song back then. How do you feel when you listen to oldies on the radio or hear "your" song? The song acts as an auditory anchor that triggers those memories and the emotions stored with them. This is a common experience. I recently experienced this firsthand.

After my mother's death last year, I chose *I'll Fly Away* as one of the songs for her memorial service. Very shortly before she died, she looked at me with good eye contact and asked, "We're about to fly away ain't we?" I answered, "Yes, mom, I believe we are. Is that okay with you?" She said, "It's okay." This was at a time when she could barely put two words together due to advanced Alzheimer's and seemed to have almost no awareness of what was happening around her, at least none that she could communicate.

A few months after my mother died, I went to see the movie *O Brother, Where Art Thou?* It is a hilarious comedy. Midway through the movie the sound track played one of the most beautiful renditions of *I'll Fly Away* that I've ever heard. Everyone around me was laughing appropriately, and I began sobbing out loud uncontrollably. My brain chemistry immediately changed to exactly what it was when I heard this song at my mother's funeral. I was overcome with emotion. The song *I'll Fly Away* will always be an auditory anchor that puts me in touch with the sorrow I feel at losing my mother, as well as my gratitude that she was able to communicate her awareness and acceptance of her death to me at such a critical time. Nothing about her physical condition could explain this. Some things go beyond the physical.

If we continue to live, we continue to add years to our chronological age. However, our beliefs about aging affect how we age.

You can see the physiological changes in your body when

you eat healthy and exercise regularly. Those changes are happening on the inside as well as the outside. Having more muscle mass increases your metabolism, strength and energy, all indicators of youth. However, there is scientific evidence that demonstrates we directly affect our physiological age not only by how we treat our bodies, but how we think. Choosing the brain chemistry for youth and vigor is available to you. It is a Super Power you possess. The suggestion is not to live in the past, but to keep the aspects of youth that serve you well, along with the wisdom you have earned.

The following is an imagery technique designed to give you that experience. You may use visual anchors such as photographs or memorabilia from your chosen time period as visual anchors.

Music from that time period can serve as effective auditory anchors. Olfactory anchors from your chosen time period can be a particular type of cologne, bath oil, or other smell good stuff. This imagery exercise is also available in CD and audiotape. Ordering information is at the back of this book.

Time Travel Imagery Exercise

Chose a particular time period that you consider to be your most optimum. Once you have chosen a particular time period, get comfortable, and relax. Take deep breathes through your nose and out your mouth until you feel your muscles in your neck and shoulders begin to relax. Slowly and gradually feel the muscle relaxation travel throughout the rest of your body.

Take your time, and allow your mind to wander through your past experiences during this time period. Tell yourself to go directly to your most positive experiences. What do you like about yourself at this age? What was important to you at this time?

Choose a particular desired state of mind that is special to you. Maybe it was excitement due to an important achievement or event, maybe it was being in love. Whatever the desired state is, relive it with all the sensory detail that you experienced when it first happened.

Pay particular attention to any physical memories in your body. As you are experiencing these physical memories, know that physical changes are occurring in your body that are in essence turning back your biological clock and improving your health.

Once you have that desired state clearly in your body and mind, give it a verbal and physical anchor. Hold that feeling for a little while, and then let it begin to subside. Before it goes, call it back again by using your anchors. Know that the more you practice this, the easier it will become to access this desired state.

Stay in this desired state for as long you are comfortable. You may want to tell yourself to carry this desired state with you into the present, and keep it with you, or have it available whenever you choose.

When you are ready, become aware of your surroundings and be in the present now.

Consider how your life would be different if you woke up tomorrow and you were your desired age and could still keep your wisdom. You may be limiting your choices in life because you believe you are too old to do something that you would do if you were in your perceived prime. Challenge these limiting beliefs, and if only for a moment, let your imagination soar.

Once you allow the conception of new ideas to form, you have planted a seed that can grow, branch out and begin to influence your life in positive directions. Even if you quickly shut this door out of a learned thought response and tell yourself that you should be "practical" and "realistic", allowing yourself even a small amount of time each day to dream big can change your life. These dreams can take the shape of plans and plans take action. *Action is the bridge between a dream and reality, but first you have to dream.*

Modern Science Anchors

As the baby boomers age, plastic surgery is an option more and more people are choosing. It may sound contradictory to endorse plastic surgery in a book that teaches natural anti-aging techniques; however, changing your outward appearance so that it matches your younger, inner spirit can be a powerful physical anchor that promotes the brain chemistry and physiological changes of youth. Thinking young can change the way you look and feel, and looking young can change the way you think and feel. It's a personal choice.

Forward Time Travel

Time travel can go both ways. You can also predict the future and gain a greater sense of control over your life and your destiny. Certainly there are life events that we have no control over. You can't predict everything in your future. However, there is much that is predictable. Since people are creatures of habit, you may already be good at predicting someone's behavior in a particular situation.

We can also predict our own behavior. The outcome of events directly reflects the choices we make. If we attempt to solve a problem today by approaching it in the same way that failed yesterday, we can predict it won't work. Sometimes we think we are trying something different, but if we take a closer look, we realize we may be doubling our efforts, but we are trying more of the same.

There are other ways to predict the future. When you set a goal, visualizing yourself achieving it can be very powerful. Athletes often use imagery to improve their performance. When you have a clear vision, then you have a clear direction set in your conscious mind. Your subconscious mind will accommodate you and follow suit.

Giving yourself clearly defined positive messages can also help your subconscious mind work for you. Your subconscious does not know the difference between your imagination and what is real. When you treat your goal achievement as a given, the other 90% of your brain will act accordingly.

When you learn to trust yourself, and your higher power, you will be open and ready and what you need will follow. Simply making a decision to be more in touch with your subconscious mind seems to give it permission to be seen and heard. You notice things that would have previously escaped you. You find you have opportunities that may have gone unrecognized. It doesn't require a lot of work or even specific learning, just a decision to be more aware and a willingness to be a more active player in your own life.

Accessing Your Subconscious Through Sleep and Dreams

As we sleep, our subconscious processes our experiences of the day and the recent past, and refuels by restoring the brain chemicals we need to function well. Without the proper rest, we may find ourselves "short a few pints". Do you frequently experience the brain chemistry "cocktail" of chronic fatigue? The remedy, of course, is adequate amounts of sleep. Six hours of *uninterrupted* sleep is a bare bones minimum to replenish the daily brain chemicals we need. The amount of sleep required to feel rested will very per individual. Most people need at least 8 hours of sleep each 24-hour period to function at their best. In *Molecules of Emotion,* Candace Pert states, "our bodies are capable of making more peptides, perfectly produced in a purified state, in one night while we sleep than all the peptide chemists who have ever lived have made in all their high-tech laboratories since 1953, when synthetic peptide production began."

Since peptides are our information carriers that act as messengers throughout our brain and bodies, you can see how important a good night's sleep is. But do we get it? For any number of reasons, most of us don't receive adequate amounts of sleep and rest. Many people have sleep disorders related to problems with emotional or physical health, medication, or simply being too busy and not making sleep a priority. There can also be family situations that interfere with your sleep, like having a new baby, children that have sleep disturbances, or caring for an elderly parent.

Information that's stored in our long-term memory isn't processed in one day or night. If our brains are already on overload from our busy, stressful lifestyles, and we don't get enough sleep to replenish our supply of brain chemicals we need to function, nor to process our experiences, what happens to us? It's a pretty safe bet that we will continue to become overloaded, more stressed, very tired, unhealthy, and our cognitive abilities, including memory, will be diminished. Is it any wonder we don't know what is going on in the other 90% of our brains? We may feel lucky to function at the 10% level!

Our subconscious mind helps us problem solve during sleep. The electrical energy patterns of your brain before sleep, during sleep and when you first awake (alpha waves) are slower and allow you a portal into your subconscious mind. Keeping a note pad or mini-tape recorder near your bed to record these thoughts and your dreams can be helpful because they tend to slip away from you as you enter the more alert state of beta waves. Verbal or mental suggestions given just before falling asleep can have a more direct impact due to this entryway into the subconscious.

Hypnotherapist, Milton H. Erickson, M.D., helped several young women grow breasts by suggesting to them while they were in a trance that their breasts would become warm and tingly and start to grow. They did not remember his suggestions, but all of them grew breasts within two months. This is believed to have worked because their subconscious minds brought about the physiological change of sending extra blood to this area (15). Dr, Bernie Seigel, author of *Love, Medicine and Miracles,* states he received a letter from a group of women who increased the size of their breasts through meditation.

The following is a list of methods to help you get in touch with your subconscious. Using these methods changes your brain chemistry by increasing endorphins and other natural pleasure chemicals.

Journaling

Reading

Drawing/art

Listening to music

Recording your dreams and thoughts just before sleep and shortly after awakening

Meditation

Psychotherapy

Positive self-talk

Getting adequate sleep/rest

Getting in touch with your spirituality

Making a decision to become more aware

Listening to your inner voice, gut instincts and intuitions

Tapping into your subconscious can open a floodgate of creativity. When we let our talents go unrecognized and ignored there can be a lingering sense of discontentment that is ill-defined. We give birth to new ideas that often never grow beyond the embryo stage before they are aborted and never have a chance to see the light of day, or we can know what they could become. The creative process can take on a life all its own. You don't need to coax it. You just need to be willing to go where it leads you.

The Super Powers of Self-Healing

The powerful effects of self-healing through the means of imagery, hypnosis, meditation and spirituality are well documented. There is no doubt that we contain healing powers within us. The human body regenerates itself continually. Depending on your beliefs, you may feel that this is a God-given gift. Regardless of your beliefs, the power our bodies have to heal is evident. We can tap into this miraculous potential to self-heal, and the techniques suggested above can be a place to start. Bring your unconscious healing powers into your conscious awareness. You can choose the brain chemistry of self-healing. You can concentrate on a particular area of your body and control physiological changes to improve your health.

Imagery has been used very successfully to help people recover from life threatening or "terminal" illness, including cancer. The type of imagery used depends on the illness and the person. Some people have visualized stopping the blood flow to a tumor. Some have visualized tumors shrinking and disappearing, or visualized warmth to an injured area to heal it. How you choose to visualize yourself healing and getting well is very individualized.

I recently used this technique to stop a recurring problem with vertigo. It is a feeling of constant motion sickness complete with dizziness and nausea. The only relief I could get was to lie down in a dark, quiet room for long periods of time. I used some of that quiet time wisely by thinking about what the dizziness reminded me of, and visualizing it.

I saw rapid, swirling, murky water like that I witnessed once during a flashflood in Oklahoma. I know that the symptoms can occur due to an inner ear problem where the ear sends signals to the brain that the body is in motion even though it is not. I visualized two "dams" one on each side of my head by my ears that would block that swirling water, or signal. Once the dams were in place the water stopped swirling and was calm, clear and peaceful, and so was I. After a few times of using this technique, the symptoms stopped altogether. Should they reappear, I'll know what to do.

Our body has a way of telling us to slow down and take better care of ourselves, and at times we are forced to listen. Use your self-healing Super Powers by creating your own imagery for your symptoms and health problems. The imagery you create will be much more effective than using someone else's ideas.

Prevention is even better than cure. Giving yourself messages to stay healthy and strong each night can help prevent illness and help your subconscious direct your conscious mind on a healthy path. As with everything else, your beliefs make the difference.

Faith and hope has its own brain chemistry and it is a healing one. Faith heals, whether that faith is in a higher power that many people call God, faith in yourself, or both. You can change your brain chemistry to that of hope and faith by using the same techniques described to access any desired state, and by exploring and developing your spiritual self.

Our immune system is a vital part of the ability to self-heal. We strengthen our immune systems by putting healthy nourishment into our bodies, not abusing or neglecting ourselves, and by utilizing our hidden Super Powers to heal ourselves physically, emotionally and spiritually. Stress is one of the most significant factors in weakening our immune systems and developing illness. Here are some other suggestions to strengthen your immune system and increase your natural endorphins, which also decreases pain:

Deep breathing

Meditation

Laughter/comedy

Vitamin C and other antioxidants

Positive touch/massage

Positive thoughts

Pleasant imagery

Giving and receiving love

Movies/books that evoke positive feelings

Spirituality

Music you find enjoyable

Physical Activity

Make the most of your gift of healing. It is a Super Power that can not only lengthen your life but, more importantly, make it worth living.

What is Your Destiny?

Do you believe in destiny? Webster's New Dictionary defines destiny as "a power which foreordains; a course of events or person's fate that is regarded as fixed by this power". Destination is defined as "a place to which a person or thing is bound; intended end of a journey." Many people believe in destiny, and many believe the power that foreordains is God, or their higher power, regardless of religious denomination. A Higher Power can have significantly different meanings depending on a person's cultural background and religious views. Most of us believe in some form of a Higher Power.

Often this belief in destiny seems to absolve some people from taking responsibility for their lives. They may take a passive stance and a "Whatever happens is meant to happen, and there is nothing I can do about it" attitude. Part of our uniqueness as human beings is free will.

We humans have the same energy ingredients as every other form of energy in the universe. This can be interpreted as having God, or our Higher Power, within us and with us at all times.

Parents can't be with their child at every moment, so, as parents, we have to equip our children with what they will need to stay safe and thrive if our attention is elsewhere. Our Higher Power equipped us well. Our grand design as humans provides us with all we will ever need, if we only come to recognize and use those innate powers.

Destiny may mean a fixed course of events we are intended to follow to fulfill our maximum purpose in life, but do we read the signs? Even more to the point, do we even see the signs? It would be difficult to travel successfully to any destination without markers, maps or road signs to help direct our way. We might end up just wandering around and getting lost. If you take the "whatever will be will be" posture, are you truly following your destiny?

Synchronicity is a term used to describe what some may call coincidence, and what others might call divine intervention. It is a timing of events that seems to direct or guide your destiny in a positive direction. If that had not happened, this wouldn't have happened. If I had not been at this place at this moment, we may have never met, and so on. When you develop an awareness of synchronicity, it seems to happen to you more and more. Actually, it has always been happening, but you may not have had a conscious awareness of it.

In *Love, Medicine and Miracles,* Dr. Bernie Siegel states, "We prepare our future by what we think and do each day. I recommend that patients keep a diary of their thoughts. As they read it later, they will see how they prepared their future by their thoughts, which then motivated their activities."

If you have kept journals from your past, you might review them and you will see the evidence of how your thinking *then* shaped your life *today*. To predict a desirable future, you can follow Dr. Siegel's suggestion and begin keeping a journal now and fill it with *facts* about your future. Your subconscious will then be better informed and can lead you in that direction.

If you are not good at keeping a journal, you might try an annual letter to yourself proclaiming what your life is going to be like over the next year. Pick approximately the same date each year, perhaps the turn of the New Year, or your birthday. Once you start doing this, even if you are not consciously thinking about it during the year, your subconscious mind is still aware of it and guiding you towards your *chosen* destiny.

If you think back over your past and look at where you are today, you can see signs or indicators that marked your direction to this point in your life.

We all know with certainty that life in our physical form is time-limited. We just don't know what the limit is. This was never brought home to us as a society so collectively as on September 11, 2001 with the terrorist attacks on the World Trade

Center and the Pentagon.

We tend to act as though there will always be a tomorrow for us and those we love, and we will have time later to do the things we want to do. If we put everything off until later how will we ever fulfill our destinies? What if we each have more than one destiny available to us?

Suppose we have Destiny Option Number One: to use our gifts to our fullest potential, live to be very old, remain healthy, happy, and productive throughout our life and make lasting contributions to others. Or, we have Destiny Option Number Two: we don't take the time or believe in ourselves enough to even recognize our gifts, self-neglect and self-abuse in ways that guarantee to make us sick and to shorten our lives, and give up on what we would like to do for ourselves and others before we even get started.

Of course, there could be many more destiny options. There may be some things that happen because they are supposed to happen, but there are many things that could happen differently if we followed the path that was intended for us.

Maybe you are on the right path, but someone you love is not. We each have our own journey. It can be difficult when you see someone you love more than you love life or yourself make choices that take them down a very treacherous road. Sometimes there is little, if anything, you can do except love them.

Where are the signs and how do you know them when you see them? Signs can be anywhere and everywhere and take many forms. It could literally be a sign on a billboard, on a bumper sticker, or something you read somewhere. A sign could be something someone says to you, or a problem they share about their life that can give you insight into yours.

You don't have to drive yourself crazy trying to read the signs of your destiny or obsessing about missing something important. Recognizing the signs is something that happens through awareness, through a decision to be open and receptive to the subconscious part of yourself, and through trusting yourself and your intuitions. There is an excellent book titled *Celestine Prophecy* that addresses these topics. When the signs are correctly read, you will know it.

One of my most significant "signs" came through an incredible woman named Marion Jacewitz, Ph.D. She was the Executive Director for the At Risk Parent Child Program in Tulsa, OK several years ago. I worked as her Administrative Assistant while I was going to college. Marion was instrumental in establishing the child abuse prevention program statewide through the state health departments. She was one woman who accomplished great things in her short life. She died of cancer at age forty leaving behind her husband and two young sons. I am still discovering things I learned from her. Her strength and influence has guided my career choices, including writing, but particularly in the treatment and prevention of physical and sexual abuse.

About seventeen years after Marion's death, Sandy Aveni, a close friend who also worked with Marion, happened to work with Marion's oldest son, Nicholas, in a job unrelated to the program. She told him many stories that helped him know his mother better. This is synchronicity at its finest. There is something to learn from each person who crosses your path, and something to give to each person who crosses yours. You may never fully know the impact you have on someone else's life.

The memories of those we've lost stay with us for the rest of our lives. All that we shared with them is stored in its entirety. When you know someone well, you can predict what he or she would say or do in most situations. Our lost loved ones can still guide us and we can still feel their love even if we can't touch their faces.

The techniques used in Virtual Reality Fantasy can be used to access any memories you want to experience, including those of lost loved ones. The brain chemistry of love and closeness you experienced when they were with you can still be experienced in the present. You can do this by accessing physical memories as well as sensory memories and using anchors such as personal belongings or photographs to recall loving times with those you have lost. It doesn't mean dwelling in the past. It can mean visiting once in a while.

The road to your destiny is clearly marked. It would be a shame if you were not paying attention. You have been given gifts you haven't unwrapped yet. Develop your Super Powers and use them for good.

Reference Books

1. Andreas, Connirae, Ph.D., and Andreas, Steve, *Heart of the Mind,* Moab, Utah, Real People Press, 1989

2. Blum, Deborah, *Sex on the Brain,* Harmonsworth Middlesex, England, Penguin Books, 1998

3. Caprio, Frank, M.D., and Berger, Joseph R., *Healing Yourself with Self-Hypnosis*, Patamus, NJ, Prentice Hall, 1998

4. Carper, Jean, *Your Miracle Brain*, New York, NY, HarperCollins Publishers Inc., 2000

5. Chopra, Deepak, M.D., *Ageless Body, Timeless Mind*, New York, NY, Harmony Books, 1993

6. Crenshaw, Theresa L., M.D., *The Alchemy of Love and Lust*, New York, NY, Pocket Books, 1996

7. Fisher, Helen E., *Anatomy of Love,* New York, Norton, 1992

8. Ford, Gillian, *Listening to Your Hormones*, Rockin, CA, Prima Publishing, 1997

9. Hayward, Susan, *You Have a Purpose – Begin It Now*, Australia, In Tune Books

10. Hooper, Judith, and Teresi, Dick, *The 3-Pound Universe*, New York, NY Jeremy P. Tarcher/Putman, 1986

11. Jensen, Eric, *The Learning Brain,* San Diego, CA, Turning Point Publishing, 1995

12. Levay, Simon, *The Sexual Brain*, Cambridge, MA, MIT Press, 1993

13. Masters, William H., *On Sex and Human Loving*, Boston, MA, Little, Brown, 1986

14. O'Connor, Joseph, and Seymour, John, *Introducing NLP*, San Francisco, CA, Thorsons, an Imprint of HarperCollins Publishers, 1995

15. Pert, Candace, *Molecules of Emotion*, New York, NY, Touchstone, 1997

16. Ramachandran, V.S., M.D., Ph.D., and Blakeslee, Sandra, *Phantoms in the Brain,* NY, Quill William Morrow, First Quill Edition, 1999

17. Sanders, Pete A., Jr., *Access Your Brain's Joy Center*, Sedona, AZ, Free Soul, 1996

18. Siegel, Bernie, S., M.D., *Love, Medicine & Miracles*, New York, NY, HarperPerennial, 1998

19. Valenstein, Elliot S., *Brain Stimulation and Motivation,* Glenview, IL, Scott, Foresman Physiological Psychology Series, 1973

20. Van Fleet, James K., *Hidden Power*, Paramus, NJ, Prentice-Hall, Inc., 1987

21. Zim, Herbert S., Ph.D., Sc.D., and Baker, Robert H., Ph.D, D.Sc, *Stars*, New York, NY, Books Publishing Company, St. Martin's Press, 1985

Reference Articles/Website

Neuroscience

22. Gold, Ian, and Stoljar, Daniel, "A Neuron Doctrine in the Philosophy of Neuroscience", *Behavioral and Brain Science*, 22(5): XXX-XXX, http://www.cogsci.soton.ac.uk/hhs/Archive/bbs.gold.html, 3/6/01

23. Madden, John, Ph.D., "Psychobiology of Mental Control"

24. Rocha do Amarai, Julio, M.D., and Sabbatini, Renato, M.E., Ph.D., "Placebo Effect: The Power of the Sugar Pill", http://www.epub.org.br/cm/n09/mente/placebo1i.htm,3/06/01

25. Delego, Jose, M., M.D., "Physical Control of the Mind", Human Pleasure Evoked by Electrical Stimulation of the Brain, http://wireheading.com/delgado/index.html, 11/26/00

26. Bozarth, Michael A., "Pleasure Systems in the Brain", 1994, http://wings.buffalo.edu/aru/ARUreport01.htm, 3/02/00

27. "Introduction to Learning", Mental Health Net, Classical Conditioning — Psychological Self-Help, http://mentalhelp.net/psyhelp/chap4/chap4d.htm, 3/06/01

Health/Diet

28. Jacobsen, Michael F., Ph.D., "Liquid Candy: How Soft Drinks are Harming American's Health", http://www.cspinet.org/sodapop/liquid_candy.htm, 6/9/01

29. National Institutes of Health, "Calcium Crisis Affects American Youth", 12/10/01, http://www.nih.gov/news/pr/decs00l//nichd_10,htm

30. National Institute on Drug Abuse, "Dopamine Receptors Implicated in Obesity", http://www.nida.nih.gov/MedAdv/ol/NRZ_1.html, 2/01/01

Transcendental Meditation

31. "Scientific Research on Transcendental Meditation and TM-SIDHI Programmes", http://www.tm.org.nz/research/defalut.asp, 5/23/01

32. "How Meditation Works", Holistic-online.com http://holisticonline.com/meditation/hol_meditation_how.htm, 5/23/01

33. "Health Problems, Addiction Research – Transcendental Meditation lowers use of cigarettes, alcohol and drugs", Internet Health Library http://www.internethealthlibrary.com/Health-problems/addictionsresearch

Sexuality

34. "Contraceptive and Sexual Implications of Disability and Illness", http://xweb.crha_health.ab.ca/chr/srh/disability.html, 5/23/01

35. Cutler, B., Friedmann E., McCoy, N.L., "Pheromone Research Information — Human Studies 1998", Arch Sex Behav, 227(1): 1-13 1998, Feb, http://www.ifnet.or.jpl~jyoti/hum-stud.html, 3/05/01

36. "Pheromone Research Information – General Information 1998", http://www.ifnet.orijp/~joyti/genfo.html , 3/05/01

37. "Female Sexual Response", Thriveonline, Oxygen Media 2000 http://www.thriveonline.aol.com/sex/women/female_sex_response/excitement.html, 11/16/00

38. "The Orgasmic Brain, http://www.pardise-engineering.com/brain/index.htm, 11/16/01

39. "Male Sexuality, Arousal and Orgasm", The-penis.com http://www.geocities.com/HotSprings/5571/malesexuality.html , 3/05/01

40. Silver, Nina, Ph.D., "The Biology of Passion: A Reichian View of Sex and Love", http://www.orgone.org/articles/ax2000nina_01.htm, 2/18/01

41. "Testosterone", Highland Pharmacy, http://www.highlandpharmacy.com/testosterone.htm, 2/18/01

42. Jelovsek, Fredrick R., M.D., "Will Testosterone Help Menopausal Symptoms?" Women's Diagnostic Cyber. http://www.wdxcyber.com/nmood10.htm, 11/26/00

43. National Institutes of Health, "Researchers Seek Women with Premature Ovarian Failure for Testosterone Replacement Study", 2-26-01, http://www.nih.gov/news/pr/feb2001/nichd_26.htm

44. Seifer, Judy, "Sexual Health", *For Women First*, August 2001

Nicotine Addiction

45. "Radioactive Tobacco", http://leda.lyceum.org/documents/radioactive_tobacco.12555.shtml , 9/18/01

46. "What Happens When You Stop Smoking", Fact Sheet No.11, ASH Organization, http://www.ash.org.uk/htm//factsheets/htm//fact//.html , 6/09/01

47. "What's in a Cigarette?" http://www.quitsmokinguk.com.what's_in_a_cigarette.htm, 5/23/01

48. Pressinger, Richard W., M.Ed., "Cigarette Smoking During Pregnancy, http://www.chem-tox.com/pregnancy/smoking.htm, 6/09/01

49. Rosen, Peg, "Why Cigarettes Can Be a Woman's Worst Enemy", 1999 http://www.cnn.com.HEALTH/Women/9911/08/women.smoking.2.wmd/index.htm, 6/09/01

50. National Institute on Drug Abuse, National Institutes of Health, "Cigarettes and Other Nicotine Products", http://www.nida.nih.gov/Infofax/tobacco.html , 6/09/01

References

51. "Cigarette's Deleterious Ingredients: Toxic Tobacco Smoke", http://downloads.members.tupad.com/medicolgal/toxicchemicals.htm, 5/23/01

52. Rowley, Christine, "Spiking Tobacco: How to Keep Smokers Hooked", Smoking Cessation, 1999, http://quitsmoking.about.com/health/quitsmoking/library/weekly/aa071999.htm, 6/09/01

53. "Just What's In a Cigarette?" http://www.quitnet.com/library/guide/Quitnet/g_what.jtm/, 6/09/01

54. Tuormaa, Tuula E., "The Adverse Effects of Tobacco Smoking on Reproduction",Foresight, http://www.surveyweb.org.uk/foresight/smoking.html , 6/09/01

55. American Heart Association, "Active and Passive Tobacco Exposure: A Serious Pediatric Health Problem", 1994, http://www.americanheart.org/scientific/statement/1994/119401.html , 6/09/01

56. "Tobacco Use: The Facts", The Daily Apple Website http://www.thedailyapple.com/target/cs/article/cs/100443.html, 6/09/01

57. "Cancer Facts and Figures", 1996 http://www.cancer.org/statistics/96cff/tobacco.htm/, 6/09/01

58. South Carolina Dept. of Alcohol and Other Drug Abuse, "Clearing the Smoke", 1996, Information Clearing House http://www.scprevents.org/web/infosite/readroom/clearing,html , 6/09/01

59. "The Sober Alcoholic's Stop Smoking Support Page, http://www.unhooked.com/nosmoke/, 6/20/01

60. "Tobacco Explained: 8. Big Tobacco and Women", 11/22/98 http://www.ash.org.uk/html/conduct/html/tobexpld8.html, 7/18/01

61. "Nicotine", Health Views, 1998, http://www.mhv.net/~donn/habitkicker/smknic.htm, 9/18/01

62. National Institute of Health, "Therapy to Help Women Reduce Their Concerns About Gaining Weight Found to Be Effective in Helping Them to Stop Smoking", 8/01/01, http://www.nih.gov/news/pr/aug2001/nida.01.htm

63. Brookhaven National Laboratory, "Therapeutic Drug Blocks Nicotine Effects on Brain Chemistry", 11/08/01, http://www.bnl.gov/bnlweb/pubaf/pr/2001/bnlpr110801.htm

64. National Institute on Drug Abuse "Quitting Smoking Harder for Women than for Men", 5/10/2001, http://www.nida.nih.gov/MedAdv/01/NR5_1a.html

65. Leshner, Alan I., Ph.D., Director, National Institute on Drug Abuse, "Parents: Nicotine Is a Real Threat to Your Kids", 1/25/01, http://www.nida.nih.gov/published_articles/nicotinethreat.html

66. Woods, Michael, "Cigarette will Deliver Dose of Radiation too", 5/00 http://www.mail_archive.com/doewatch@egroups.com/mgg00277.html, 9/18/01

67. National Cancer Institute, "Low-Tar Cigarettes: Evidence Does Not Indicate a Benefit to Public Health", 11/27/01 http://newscenter.cancer.gov/pressreleases/lowtar.html

Alcohol and Other Addictions

68. Florida Alcohol & Drug Abuse Association: Resources, "Just the Facts: Alcohol", http://www.fadaa.org/resources/justfact/alcohol.html, 6/22/01

69. "Alcohol", Neuroscience for Kids, http://faculty.washington.educ/chudler.alco.html, 6/22/01

70. Nash, Madeline, "Addicted", *Time*, May 5,1997

71. "Overview of Alcohol Related Problems", Columbia University College of P & S Complete Home Medical Guide http://ccpmcnet_columbia.edu/texts/guide/hmg06_0003.html, 6/22/01

72. Driesen, Jacob L., Ph.D., "Brain and Addiction" http://www.driesen.com/brain_and_addiction.htm, 5/23/01

73. National Institutes of Health, "Neuroimaging Identifies Brain Regions Possibly Involved in Alcohol Craving", 4/12/01 http://www.nih.gov/news/pr/apr2001/niaaa-12.htm

74. Stocker, Steven, National Institute of Drug Abuse, "Studies Link Stress and Drug Addiction", *Research Findings*, Volume14, Number 1, April, 1999, http://www.nida.nih.gov/NIDA_Notes/NNVol14nl/stress.html

75. National Institute on Drug Abuse, "Potential Medication Can Reduce Effects of Smoked Marijuana in Humans", 4-12/01, http://www.nida.nih.gov/MedAdv/01/NR4-12.html

76. Leshner, Alan I., "Addiction Is a Brain Disease", Issues in science and Technology Online, Spring 2001, http://www.nap.edu/issues/17.3/leshner.htm

Frances Williams Duncan, LCSW, is a licensed psychotherapist in private practice with Positive Solutions Counseling Center in Largo, Florida. She received her MSSW from the University of Louisville in 1987, and then completed a two-year externship in Brief Strategic and Solution Focused Therapy at the Dayton Institute of Family Therapy in Dayton, Ohio. She has specialized training in Neuro-Linguistic Programming, sexual abuse treatment, and advanced hypnotherapy.

In her 14 years of clinical experience, Ms. Duncan has primarily focused her extensive training and experience on treating children who have been physically and/or sexually abused and their families. Ms. Duncan is experienced in play therapy and works with special needs children. Her practice includes working with adults as well as children.

Ms. Duncan is presently offering **weight loss and smoking cessation groups based on the Physical Memory Accessing techniques** presented in *Developing Your Super Powers*.

Online consultation is available on a **limited basis** to answer questions about Physical Memory Accessing and help you develop your Super Powers. Go to **www.innergalaxies.com**

EXPERIENTIAL WORKSHOPS AND SEMINARS

Frances Duncan, LCSW, conducts Experiential Workshops and Seminars based on the revolutionary new techniques of Physical Memory Accessing. Physical Memory Accessing techniques allow you to access the pleasure systems of your brain with thought. You develop the ability to release your brain's pleasure chemicals like dopamine, serotonin, and endorphins, therefore, giving you the ability to choose your brain chemistry and states of mind naturally.

These pleasure chemicals are what we seek when we fall "in love", have sex, smoke cigarettes, use alcohol and/or other drugs, compulsively overeat, and take prescribed medication for pain, depression and anxiety. When you access the pleasure systems of your brain with thought, you learn how to eliminate addictive behaviors without putting any harmful substances into your body.

Physical Memory Accessing is based in neuroscience and is related to how the brain works, how memory is stored and retrieved, how our senses of sight, sound, touch, smell and taste operate and how we learn. Specific techniques of Physical Memory Accessing, called Physical Memory Orgasms, allow women to have unlimited orgasms, at will, without sexual stimulation or fantasy. Men can extend and enhance their sexual experiences and orgasms.

The benefits of Physical Memory Accessing include: reducing trauma responses, effective weight loss, having the pleasurable brain chemistry of smoking without cigarettes, staying (or returning) to the "in love" stage of a romantic relationship indefinitely, self-healing, reverse aging, activating your motivation, natural pain relief, decreasing/eliminating depression and anxiety, choosing your moods, and much more.

Experiential Workshops and Seminars specifically for smoking cessation and weight loss are offered. Training is available for professionals interested in expanding their resources and further developing their skills to help clients. For more information call toll free 877-434-0005 or on the web at www.innergalaxies.com

Information and order forms follow for:

DEVELOPING YOUR SUPER POWERS WORKBOOK

YOU STILL FEEL MY LOVE CD

DEVELOPING YOUR SUPER POWERS GUIDED IMAGERY CD's/TAPES

Additional Books —
DEVELOPING YOUR SUPER POWERS

DEVELOPING YOUR SUPERPOWERS WORKBOOK

The *Developing Your Super Powers Workbook*, by Frances Williams Duncan, LCSW, is filled with unique Physical Memory Accessing techniques to assist you in developing your Super Powers. The *Developing Your Super Powers Workbook* is designed to complement and enhance the skills you learned from reading *Developing Your Super Powers*.

You will be provided with easy to follow step-by-step activities and instructions to help you better achieve your goals. For more information, or to order the *Developing Your Super Powers Workbook* online, go to www.innergalaxies.com. You can also order by mail. Send your order form to:

Inner Galaxies Press
P.O. Box 2298
Tarpon Springs, FL 34688-2298
Toll Free 877-434-0005

DEVELOPING YOUR SUPER POWERS WORKBOOK
Order Form

Name _____

Address _____

City _____ State _____ Zip Code _____

Phone _____ E-Mail Address (optional) _____ Fax _____

Quantity _____ @ $14.00 each = $ _____

Fla. Residents Add 7% Sales Tax _____
S/H First Item   4.00
Plus $.75 S/H Each Additional _____
Total _____

Type of Payment: Check – Credit Card – Money Order

Credit Card # _____ Card Type _____

Expiration Date _____

Signature _____

Mail to: Inner Galaxies Press
P.O. Box 2298
Tarpon Springs, FL 34688-2298

You can also order online at:
www.innergalaxies.com
or call Toll Free 877-434-0005

Anyone who has recently lost a parent, or is caring for an aging parent, may gain some comfort from the heartfelt CD, *You Still Feel My Love*. Frances Williams Duncan, LCSW, wrote the lyrics while she was caring for her terminally ill mother, Mary Kerr, who suffered from advanced Alzheimer's disease. She took the poem to a very talented and dear lifetime friend, Donnie King, and asked him to put it to music for her mother's memorial service. The result is *You Still Feel My Love*.

The Hospice team that provided their tireless and dedicated care for Mary thought many others could benefit from this song. So for that, and in tribute to Mary Frances Kerr, the song is now available. **If you would like to hear a portion of the song, log on to www.innergalaxies.com.** You can get your own copy by mail order using the attached CD order form, or **order online at www.innergalaxies.com.**

YOU STILL FEEL MY LOVE
CD Order Form

Name _____

Address _____

City _____ State _____ Zip Code _____

Phone _____ E-Mail Address (optional) _____ Fax _____

Quantity _____ @ $3.98 each = $ _____
Fla. Residents Add 7% Sales Tax _____
S/H First Item   2.00
Add $.50 S/H Each Additional _____

Total _____

Type of Payment: Check – Credit Card – Money Order

Credit Card # _____ Card Type _____

Expiration Date _____

Signature _____

Mail to: Inner Galaxies Press
P.O. Box 2298
Tarpon Springs, FL 34688-2298
**You can hear a portion of the CD and order online at:
www.innergalaxies.com
or call toll free 877-434-0005**

DEVELOPING YOUR SUPER POWERS

DEVELOPING YOUR SUPER POWERS
GUIDED IMAGERY CD's/TAPES

CD's and Audiotapes of guided imagery exercises presented in *Developing Your Super Powers* are available to help you better learn the techniques and further develop *your* Super Powers.

#	Title	Cost
SP1 – **Physical Memory Accessing and Physical Memory Orgasms**		$9.00
SP2 – **Virtual Reality Fantasy**		$7.00
SP3 – **Diluting Sexual Abuse Trauma Responses**		$7.00
SP4 - **Super Power Weight Loss**		$7.00
SP5 – **Super Power Smoking Cessation**		$7.00
SP6 – **Time Travel and Reverse Aging**		$7.00
SP7 – **Your Self-Healing Super Powers**		$7.00
SP8 – **Set of all seven tapes ($6.00 savings)**		$45.00

To order by mail, send your order form to:
Inner Galaxies Press
P.O. Box 2298
Tarpon Springs, FL 34688-2298
To order online: www.innergalaxies.com
or call toll free 877-434-0005

DEVELOPING YOUR SUPER POWERS
GUIDED IMAGERY CD's/TAPES
Order Form

Name

Address

City   State   Zip Code

Phone   E-Mail Address (optional)   Fax

Product #	Title	Quantity	Total Price
		Subtotal	

CD's ☐   Fla. Residents Add 7% Sales Tax _____
Tapes ☐   S/H First Item   2.00
               Add $.50 S/H Each Additional _____
               TOTAL _____

Type of Payment: Check – Credit Card – Money Order

Credit Card #_____ Card Type_____

Expiration Date_____

Signature_____

Mail to: Inner Galaxies Press
P.O. Box 2298
Tarpon Springs, FL 34688-2298
To order online:
www.innergalaxies.com
or call toll free 877-434-0005

DEVELOPING YOUR SUPER POWERS

DEVELOPING YOUR SUPER POWERS
Order Form

Name _____

Address _____

City _____ State _____ Zip Code _____

Phone _____ E-Mail Address (optional) _____ Fax _____

Quantity _____ @ $15.00 each = $ _____

                Fla. Residents Add 7% Sales Tax _____
                              S/H First Item   4.00
                  Plus $.75 S/H Each Additional _____
                                          Total _____

Type of Payment: Check – Credit Card – Money Order

Credit Card # _____ Card Type _____

Expiration Date _____

Signature _____

Mail to: Inner Galaxies Press
        P.O. Box 2298
        Tarpon Springs, FL 34688-2298

                You can also order online at:
                    www.innergalaxies.com
              or call Toll Free 877-434-0005

DEVELOPING YOUR SUPER POWERS

READER SURVEY

DEVELOPING YOUR SUPER POWERS

PHENOMENAL MIND POWERS YOU DON'T KNOW YOU HAVE

Sharing your experiences using the Physical Memory Accessing Techniques will help us refine the techniques to better help people like yourself who wish to achieve their utmost potential. Thank you for your time in filling out and mailing this anonymous form to the address listed at the end of the survey.

Gender: M F   Marital Status _____ Age ____
Sexual Orientation _____
   (heterosexual, homosexual, bi-sexual) (optional)

Section 1.

1. **Do you have any health problems or physical limitations? If so, what are they? How does this affect your sexual functioning?**

2. Do you have any problems with perimenopause, menopause, hysterectomy, viropause or other physical problems that affect your hormone levels? What are your symptoms?

3. Are you taking any medications or hormone replacement therapy that affects your sexual functioning? If so, please list what type of medication and the effects.

Section 2.

4. Did you find any limiting beliefs that affected your orgasmic potential and sexuality? Briefly summarize.

5. What is your current Maximum Orgasmic Experience (MOE)? What was your MOE before using the PMOs techniques?

6. Did you experience Physical Memory Orgasms (PMOs) using the techniques in this book? If so, to what degree, and in what time frame? Briefly describe your experience using the PMOs techniques.

7. What was your experience using Virtual Reality Fantasy (VRF)?

8. Do you have a history of sexual abuse? If so, please describe your experiences using the techniques to dilute your trauma responses.

9. How has developing your Super Powers affected your relationships?

Section 3.

10. Describe your experiences using the Super Power techniques for weight loss and healthy eating? What were your results?

11. What food patterns/associations did you find that have most affected your eating habits?

12. Are/were you a smoker? What were your experiences using the Super Power techniques to stop smoking? Please share any stop smoking tips you know.

13. Do you have an alcohol or other substance abuse problem? Describe your experience using the Super Power techniques to stop drinking or using.

Section 4.

14. Share any unique experiences tapping into your subconscious and expanding your Super Powers.

15. What were your experiences with self-healing?

16. Please share any of your experiences that you feel would be helpful to others.

Add additional sheets if needed. Include contact information if you choose.

Comments:

Mail to: Inner Galaxies Press
P.O. Box 2298
Tarpon Springs, FL 34688

You can also complete the survey online at:
www.innergalaxies.com

DEVELOPING YOUR SUPER POWERS